Methuen Drama Modern Classics

Methuen Drama's *Modern Classics* series showcases landmark plays from around the world. Drawing on the *Modern Plays* series, which launched in 1959, *Modern Classics* celebrates plays from the contemporary repertoire by world-leading dramatists and presents their work in a definitive edition, alongside new introductions by leading scholars and industry professionals. With writers such as Pulitzer Prize-winners Jackie Sibblies Drury, Ayad Akhtar and David Mamet through to Lucy Prebble, Katori Hall and Caryl Churchill, *Modern Classics* are ideal for students and anyone wanting to deepen their knowledge of the plays that form part of the modern dramatic canon.

Enron

W0232772

'**The political theatre of the 21st century has arrived, in some style.**' *The Times*

The most infamous scandal in corporate history. The most vilified figures in the financial world. The most audacious (and destructive) display of greed history has ever seen.

Charting the notorious rise and fall of the eponymous company and its founding partners Ken Lay and Jeffrey Skilling, Lucy Prebble's *Enron* is a pulse-racing and rage-inducing parable, exploring the limits of greed . . . or lack thereof.

Mixing classical tragedy with savage comedy, *Enron* is published in Methuen Drama's Modern Classics series, featuring a new introduction by Natasha Tripney.

Lucy Prebble is a writer for film, television, games and theatre. She was executive producer and writer on the BAFTA, Golden Globe and Emmy award-winning HBO drama *Succession*, for which she has also won a WGA and a PGA Award. She is the writer and co-creator of *I Hate Suzie* and *I Hate Suzie Too* which was nominated for five BAFTAs including Best Drama, Best Writer and Best Actress and won her the Royal Television Society Award for Best Writer. She is also the creator and writer of the TV series *Secret Diary of a Call Girl* (ITV/Showtime).

For theatre, Lucy had a rewritten version of her award-winning play, *The Effect*, at the National Theatre, directed by Jamie Lloyd, which then transferred to The Shed in New York. She wrote the political and emotional meta-thriller *A Very Expensive Poison* which was a sell-out, five star hit for the Old Vic in 2019 and was Olivier nominated for Best New Play. She is the writer of the infamous *Enron*, a hugely successful piece about the infamous corporate fraud, which transferred to the West End after sell-out runs at both the Royal Court and Chichester Festival Theatre. Her first play, *The Sugar Syndrome* (2003) won her the George Devine Award and was performed at the Royal Court.

Enron

Lucy Prebble

With an introduction by Natasha Tripney

methuen | drama

LONDON · NEW YORK · OXFORD · NEW DELHI · SYDNEY

METHUEN DRAMA
Bloomsbury Publishing Plc
50 Bedford Square, London, WC1B 3DP, UK
1385 Broadway, New York, NY 10018, USA
29 Earlsfort Terrace, Dublin 2, Ireland

BLOOMSBURY, METHUEN DRAMA and the Methuen Drama logo
are trademarks of Bloomsbury Publishing Plc

First published in Great Britain by Methuen Drama in 2009
This Modern Classics edition published in 2024

Cover design: Ben Anslow

A catalogue record for this book is available from the British Library.

A catalog record for this book is available from the Library of Congress.

ISBN: PB: 978-1-3504-3088-4
ePDF: 978-1-3504-3090-7
eBook: 978-1-3504-3089-1

Series: Modern Classics

Typeset by Newgen KnowledgeWorks Pvt. Ltd., Chennai, India

To find out more about our authors and books visit www.bloomsbury.com
and sign up for our newsletters.

Contents

Introduction

Theatre has never had an easy relationship with the corporate world. Perhaps out of a faint sense of distaste, the boardroom and the trading floor are spaces into which playwrights don't often venture. Lucy Prebble's play *Enron*, originally staged in 2009, thrillingly made the case that these spaces are inherently theatrical. She took material that in less skilled hands could have been dry and talky and turned it into something propulsive, kinetic and, ultimately, tragic.

The cataclysmic demise of the energy company Enron was, at the time, the largest bankruptcy in American history. Founded in 1985 in Houston, Texas, Enron was a gas pipeline company that gradually transformed itself, through a process of diversification, into an enormous trading enterprise, before collapsing spectacularly. It declared bankruptcy in 2001, having accrued debts of $38 billion.

Prebble grasped that there was something almost Shakespearean about this story of corporate ambition and overreach. She grasped that CEOs are our culture's kings. They are the men (and they are still mostly men) capable of reshaping the world, whose power plays and sense of exceptionalism have a global impact, their decisions capable of affecting millions of lives.

Enron presents a vision of the company as empire, 'In the past, folks thought that the basic unit of society would be the state or the church or . . . the political party. But we now know it's The Company', explains Enron's hands-off founder Ken Lay, played by Tim Pigott-Smith, his steeliness concealed beneath an affable Texan exterior.

Jeffrey Skilling, Enron's COO, is its emperor. He clambers to the top of the corporate pole, driven by his conviction that he is one of 'the smartest guys in the room', far cleverer than everyone else, capable of seeing what others can't see and doing what others can't do. He finds the idea of a company that merely supplies energy maddeningly unambitious and limiting. His initial idea is to trade in energy as well as supply it. But he doesn't stop there. His dreams expand to include the burgeoning video-on-demand market and even the weather. Under Skilling Enron was no longer tethered to 'things you can touch', but to the abstract and intangible. 'We're not just an energy company, we're a powerhouse for ideas', he declares. Enron was an empire built on air, an exercise in illusion, where projected profits were treated as if they were reality, while the truth was shunted into the shadows.

Outburst

Enron was almost a musical. That was the original pitch with which Prebble approached Rupert Goold, then artistic director of Headlong. A musical about corporate corruption and financial scandal. (This was some years before *Hamilton* grappled with US economic policy through the medium of hip-hop.) Goold thought the story of Enron's demise had more in keeping with a classical tragedy; arguably something of this original idea remains in the play's DNA.

A co-production between Headlong and the Royal Court, *Enron* had its world premiere at Chichester's Minerva Theatre in July 2009. Goold's production was one of flamboyance and dazzle, but it was also emotionally layered. Samuel West – a captivating Hamlet in Stephen Pimlott's 2001 production for the RSC – humanized Enron's golden boy Skilling, charting his transformation from something of a schlub, a man not wholly at ease in his own skin, to an almost Messiah-like figure, a demi-god, seemingly incapable of error and intoxicated by his own self-mythology. Skilling knew that to become a leader one must play the role and look the part. He gets corrective laser eye surgery. He hits the gym, hones his body. West deftly conveyed this external manifestation of his rampant overconfidence, which Prebble captured in the text.

Prebble was immersed in the world of business from a young age. Her father worked in a software company – the play is dedicated to him – and her siblings are management consultants. This is terrain she understands, and that comes across. *Enron* is a play of refreshing textual density. There are a lot of complex financial concepts which it needs the audience to grasp, but Prebble excels at delivering this information in ways that are both digestible and, at the same time, either drive the narrative forward or reveal something about the characters.

It helps that Enron's top dogs like nothing more than explaining their ideas to those they consider their intellectual inferiors. When we are first introduced to Skilling, he is aghast that some of the people at the party he's attending don't appreciate the brilliance of his mark-to-market strategy. 'It doesn't kill you? Everyone standing around celebrating their ignorance', he says before proceeding to explain it to the room. In detail.

Similarly, Enron's CFO-to-be Andy Fastow (played with fitting intensity by Tom Goodman-Hill), really, really wants to impress upon Skilling just how smart his scheme to buy underperforming stock is. He describes these financial entities as raptors, after the small but intelligent dinosaurs in Spielberg's *Jurassic Park*, and desperately needs not just his boss's approval but his affirmation (it's a dynamic that viewers of *Succession*, of which Prebble is a key part of the writing team and executive producer, will recognize – Fastow comes across like one of Logan Roy's offspring, only less fucked and infinitely more competent). Fastow even names one of his children Jeffrey, so in thrall is he. Fastow then goes on to name LJM, the company he creates to hide Enron's growing debts, after his wife and children, indirectly naming it after Skilling too.

The most telling and effective expository scene takes place between Skilling and his young daughter. For all his terminology-thick explanations of financial models, a child's questioning forces him to distil things, the recurring question echoing Enron's own advertisements, forever asking: why?

Skilling   I have to check the stock price.

Daughter   Why?

Skilling   Because that's how Daddy knows how much he's worth.

Daughter   Why?

Skilling   Because the market tells me.

In another scene, Skilling and his daughter play a game, one it seems they play often, in which he uses a stack of dollar bills to teach her to count. He asks her to imagine how long it would take to count out a million dollars at a dollar a second. It's a simple but brilliantly effective device, allowing the audience to visualize the enormity of the sums being discussed. It would take eleven days to get to a million dollars; to count a billion dollars that way, he tells her, it would take him thirty-two years.

If the play were just a righteously angry account of corporate wrongdoing and capitalism run amok, it wouldn't be half as compelling. Prebble makes the world these characters inhabit alluring and exciting. She captures the adrenalized environment and atmosphere of excess. She makes its glamour tangible. You grasp how easy it must have been to get swept up in it, to believe in Skilling's vision. 'There's not much point in writing about a financial bubble unless you want to spend time within that bubble', she said in an interview with Michael Billington at the time.[1]

Throughout the play, information comes at you fast, whether it's ping-ponging back and forth between characters or delivered in chorus form, by traders moving in formation, but, as Billington observed in his *Guardian* review, 'Everything is made visually apprehensible.'[2] Prebble's text gave Goold permission to be playful and Goold delivered, aided by Anthony Ward's set ribboned by the electronic stock price ticker, Jon Driscoll's video design, and Mark Henderson's inventive lighting, all columns of streaming green. The traders move to Scott Ambler's throbbing choreography. Fastow's raptors take the form of suited men with dinosaur heads, red eyes glinting ominously. The Lehman Brothers are a conjoined figure in an outsized overcoat and the Enron board is populated by blind mice. There are light-sabres and even a ventriloquist's dummy, the latter standing in for accountants Arthur Andersen. (In spite of Enron's poor accounting practices, Arthur Andersen signed off on the corporate reports for years.) Yet, this highly stylized, multimedia approach – 'a hi-tech danse macabre', according to the *Observer*'s Susannah Clapp – never comes at the expense of the human element of the play.[3] It remains emotionally grounded.

Conquest

Following its opening in Chichester, the play transferred to the Jerwood Downstairs at the Royal Court later that same year. A West End run at the Noël Coward Theatre duly followed in 2010, the stage getting bigger at every step of the journey.

This was only Prebble's second play. Her debut full-length work *The Sugar Syndrome* was smaller in scale but similarly fearless in terms of where it was willing to venture. Charting the complicated friendship between seventeen-year-old Dani, a recovering anorexic, and Tim, a paedophile, it approached its subject with empathy and wit.

Like *The Sugar Syndrome*, *Enron* is often unexpectedly funny. It's a bleak, hard kind of humour, but it's funny all the same. The play accurately captures the hyper-masculine workplace culture of the time. The intense maleness of these spaces is thrown into sharper focus by the presence of Claudia Roe (a cool, collected Amanda Drew in a hot pink suit). As a female executive, Roe doesn't just play the same game as the guys, she excels at the game. She rides into Enron's big millennium party on a Harley. But the play also acknowledges that, for her, the rules are subtly different.

Unlike Skilling, Fastow and Enron founder Lay, who are fictionalized versions of their real-life counterparts, the character of Roe is an amalgam, standing in for several women in the Enron story. She's a plausible portrait of a woman navigating a testosterone-drenched corporate environment. She is comfortable taking up space and capable of getting under Skilling's skin, but this makes her vulnerable. She reminds Skilling that he's human, and he cannot stand for that.

While Fastow at times seems besotted with Skilling, it's Roe who actually fucks him. In a key early scene, we see Roe and Skilling engaging in post-coital power play, with him absorbing the fact that they're both vying for the same role in the company just as she wipes a rivulet of his ejaculate from her leg. Prebble has always been an insightful chronicler of female sexuality. *I Hate Suzie*, Prebble's feverish comedy co-created with Billie Piper, which details the fallout when intimate pictures of a celebrity end up online, devotes a whole episode to the title character's sexual fantasies and her difficulty disentangling them from internalized patriarchal ideas about desire. Sex is part of Roe's weaponry and yet that doesn't undermine her ability as a businesswoman.

While Skilling is a magnetic figure, someone to whom people listened, even at the expense of their own growing misgivings – a skill so many men in positions of power possess – Prebble also shows us the hairline cracks in his facade. In that same *Guardian* article, she drew a parallel between Skilling and the character of Andrew Undershaft, the arms manufacturer in George Bernard Shaw's

Major Barbara, and lawyer Roy Cohn in Tony Kushner's *Angels in America*. These are both, in many ways, morally repugnant men with whom it is still on some dramatic level possible to empathize. To this end, she shows us Skilling's soft spots, his weaknesses, his anxieties: all well camouflaged but nonetheless visible.

Commerce

Enron follows a classic three act structure, with each act further broken down into a series of titled scenes. The titles set the tone: An Unholy Partnership, An Orgy of Speculation.

While the first act of the play focuses on the upward and out-wards trajectory of the company, the second act shows the beginning of the company's disintegration. The raptors have grown stronger, smarter and scarier, the first act having closed with Fastow, with delicious inevitability, referring to one as a 'clever girl'. Enron has begun to purge those viewed as threats – Roe is defenestrated despite her protestations that her division is one that consistently delivers – and the company's employees 'from the mailroom up' are offered stock options, an almost throwaway act that would prove devastating. At the same time, Skilling is waking up to the fact that the company has a cash issue, to the tune of four billion dollars. 'We're the world's most innovative company. How can we not find four billion dollars?' asks Fastow. This all plays out against the tension of the 2000 American presidential election (in a scene that at times foreshadows the 'America Decides' episode of *Succession*) as America elects George W. Bush. With a Texan in the White House, they can – briefly – breathe again.

Prebble is alert to the patterns of behaviour to which men of Skilling's status are prone. There is a delusion known as illusory control in which a person thinks they can shape outcomes to their liking even when they can't; Skilling clings to the idea that he can somehow steer Enron away from the pit into which it is about to plummet by force of will alone. He does not believe that someone of his abilities can fail. He goes on an anti-regulatory rant based not on ideology but because he believes he's inherently better than the 'bottom of the barrel, frat party, no-nothing fucks' who work in government.

With the end fast approaching, despite this unwavering self-belief, Skilling desperately needs others to appreciate his cleverness. It's all he has left. As a security guard searches an increasingly paranoid Skilling's office for bugs, he repeatedly tries to explain to the man Enron's next proposed shift into weather derivatives; he needs to have his brilliance reflected in the awed reactions of others.

Affluence

The US production of *Enron*, once again directed by Goold, opened on Broadway's Broadhurst Theatre in 2010, starring Norbert Butz in the role of Jeffrey Skilling. It's fair to say the American response to *Enron* was more muted, or at least more mixed, than its British reception. Here was a British play about one of the US's biggest corporate scandals framed against a backdrop of the ascendance of Bush and the still-raw horror of 9/11. The *New York Times'* Ben Brantley was sniffily dismissive.[4] US critic David Cote – a champion of the play – attributes this response in part to US critics being less comfortable with its post-dramatic tactics and willingness to embrace ambiguity, though it's hard to completely shake the suspicion that, at least on some level, the US critical response stemmed from some subliminal unease about the fact that a young British woman had taken it upon herself to dissect this American scandal and, with it, the machinery of American capitalism.[5] Still, it was nominated for four Tonys including one for Stephen Kunken who played Fastow in the US production.

The third act of the play details the collapse of Enron, the trial in which Skilling was convicted on nineteen counts of securities fraud and wire fraud, and the human cost which saw many Enron employees stripped of their life savings, leaving them with nothing. Prebble shows us Skilling brought low, stumbling drunk in the streets and facing a lengthy prison sentence, but while Fastow holds his hands up, and wants it on the record that he admitted what he did was wrong, Skilling still insists he only did what was required of him. Right and wrong aren't even the right terms in which to talk about what happened at Enron. This is not a moral issue; it is the nature of the system to try and game it. The 'only difference between me and the people judging me is that they weren't smart enough to do what we did', he concludes.

The Enron scandal would lead to new regulations surrounding the accuracy of financial reporting for publicly traded companies. The Sarbanes-Oxley Act was created to impose harsh penalties for destroying, altering or fabricating financial records. Prebble would go on to write *A Very Expensive Poison* (2019), a similarly formally adventurous work based on Luke Harding's book about the poisoning of Alexander Litvinenko. Reading it now, with Russia's war with Ukraine ongoing, it has the feel of an alarm bell being sounded.

Written in the aftermath of the financial crash, *Enron* is also a warning. While the story of Enron's downfall and its consequences had already been documented journalistically – in Bethany Mclean and Peter Elkin's *The Smartest Guys in the Room*, among others – and on film, Prebble not only understood the theatrical potential of this story of corporate misdirection but also found the ideal theatrical language with which to tell it.

Natasha Tripney

Notes

1   Michael Billington, 'Making a Drama out of the Economic Crisis', *The Guardian*, 14 September 2009.
2   Michael Billington, 'Review: *Enron*', *The Guardian*, 23 September 2009.
3   Susannah Clapp, 'Theatre Reviews: *Enron, The Black Album, Dreams of Violence*', *The Observer*, 26 July 2009.
4   Ben Brantley, 'Titans of Tangled Finances Kick Up Their Heels Again', *The New York Times*, 27 April 2010.
5   David Cote, 'Why Doesn't Broadway Love *Enron*?', *The Guardian*, 29 April 2010.

Enron

Enron premiered in a Headlong Theatre, Chichester Festival Theatre and Royal Court production at the Minerva Theatre, Chichester, on 11 July 2009. The first performance in London was at the Royal Court Jerwood Theatre Downstairs, Sloane Square, London, on 17 September 2009. The cast was as follows:

News Reporter	Gillian Budd
Lehman Brother, Trader	Peter Caulfield
Security Officer, Trader	Howard Charles
Trader	Andrew Corbett
Claudia Roe	Amanda Drew
Congresswoman, Business Analyst, Irene Gant	Susannah Fellows
Arthur Andersen, Trader	Stephen Fewell
Lehman Brother, Trader	Tom Godwin
Andy Fastow	Tom Goodman-Hill
Lou Pai, Senator Hewitt, News Reporter, Prostitute	Orion Lee
Ken Lay	Eleanor Matsuura
(Enron Chairman/CEO)	Tim Pigott-Smith
Ramsay, Trader	Ashley Rolfe
Jeffrey Skilling	Samuel West
Daughter	Cleo Demetriou, Ellie Hopkins
Lawyer, Trader	Trevor White

All other parts played by members of the company.

Director Rupert Goold
Designer Anthony Ward
Lighting Designer Mark Henderson
Composer and Sound Designer Adam Cork
Video and Projection Designer Jon Driscoll
Choreographer Scott Ambler
Enron transferred to the Noël Coward Theatre, London, on 16 January 2010, and opened on Broadway at the Broadhurst Theatre on 27 April 2010, presented by Matthew Byam Shaw, Act, Caro Newling for Neal Street, Jeffrey Richards and Jeffrey Frankel.

Prologue

The eerie, mechanical sound of singing. It is the word 'WHY' from Enron commercials.
Three suited individuals enter, finding their way with white sticks. They have the heads of mice.
Over which, the commercial's voice of:

Jeffrey Skilling (*V.O.*)   Enron Online will change the market. It is creating an open, transparent market place that replaces the dark, blind system that existed. It is real simple. If you want to do business, you push the button. We're trying to change the world.

The three mice-men have wandered across the stage, feeling their way with the sticks. Perhaps one turns and seems to stare at us.

A single bright light sharply illuminates **The Lawyer**.

Lawyer (*to us*)   I'm a lawyer and I'm one of the few who makes money in times like these. When businesses fail, when unemployment rises, marriages break down and men jump to their deaths. Somebody. Divides up. The money. At times like this we're exposed to how the world really works. (I could explain to you how it works but, I don't have the time and you don't have the money.) Every so often, someone comes along and tries to change that world. Can one man do that? We look at some and pray to God they can't. But, when things get desperate, we find ourselves 'A Great Man', look up to him and demand he change things.

Hypocrites. Within every great man there's a buried risk. The guy I know tried to change the world was the man behind the corporate crime that defined the end of the twentieth century, and cast a shadow over this one. Now as a lawyer I choose my words carefully. So when we tell you his story, you should know it could never be *exactly* what happened. But we're gonna put it together and sell it to you as the truth. And when you look at what happened here, and everything that came afterward, that seems about right.

Here, in the beating heart of the economic world: America. In the heart of America, Texas. And in the heart of Texas, Houston. There was a company.

Act One

Scene One – Mark to Market Party – 1992

A PARTY in a small office at Enron. Present are:

Employees *drinking champagne.*

Claudia Roe – *a blonde woman (40) in a short skirt – enters. She sticks close to:* –

Ken Lay – *an easy, short, convivial man (60s), greeting and acknowledging every employee with practised Southern hospitality.*

Andy Fastow *is a nervy, lupine guy, circling, with an unsettling grin (30s).*

Fastow *is on the outskirts, of the group of* **Employees**, *ingratiating himself.*

Roe *and* **Lay** *sweep around the room.*

Employee (*to* **Roe**)   I loved your speech, by the way.

Employee 2   Really great speech.

Roe   Oh, thank you so much.

Fastow   Quite a party.

Employee   I beg your pardon?

Lay   (How you doing. Good to see you.)

Fastow (*one eye on* **Lay**)   Just. It's great news. About mark to market.

Employee 2   Oh, the accounting system.

Employee   We just came down for the champagne.

Elsewhere:

Roe   Should we expect a speech from you, sir?

Lay   No, Claudia, I don't think we need ourselves another speech right now. Informality. Colleagues enjoying themselves.

Back at the group **Fastow** *is trying to break into:*

Fastow   Look, even Ken Lay's here.

Employee   Yeah.

Fastow   You think he plays golf?

Employee   I don't know(!)

Lay *magnanimously   greets   another   couple   of   starstruck* **Employees**.

Fastow   Where's the guy who put this thing together?

Employee 2   What do you mean?

Fastow   Jeff Skilling.

Employee   Never heard of him.

Fastow   The mark to market guy.

Employee 2   No idea.

Fastow   Maybe he's not a big party guy.

Employee   Maybe you'd get along(!)

Fastow   Actually I always thought we would.

Lay   Have I met the mark to market guy?

Roe   Jeff Skilling. I don't know where he is.

Lay   I've only got a half hour here. Make sure I shake his hand.

Outside the party, **Skilling** *straightens his suit, his hair. He's a bespectacled, overweight, balding accountant. He takes a deep breath.*

Skilling *enters the party and finds himself a drink for confidence.*

Fastow   You can't get Lay away from Claws there. It's like she's his carer.

Employee   Why don't you go talk to him?

Fastow   Yeah. You think I should?

Employee   I think you should.

Fastow   He's just a guy, I'm a guy.

Beat.

Yeah. This is how things happen.

Employee   You go girl(!)

Roe (*noticing* **Skilling**)   There he is.

Roe *goes over to collect* **Skilling**.

Fastow *strides over to introduce himself to* **Lay**.

Roe   Jeff, come over. Ken Lay.

Skilling   'Hi, how are you?'

Roe (*sarcastic*)   'Hi, how are you.'

Ken Lay.

Fastow   Hi there, Mr Lay.

Lay   You're not Jeff Skilling, / by any chance –

Fastow   No sir, I wish I was, I'm Andy –

Lay   Andy, Andy Fastow.

Fastow   Yes sir!

Lay   I make a point of knowing people, son.

Roe *drags* **Skilling** *over to* **Lay**.

Roe   Ken –

Lay *slaps* **Skilling** *on the back.*

Lay   Here's the guy! Jeffrey 'mark to market' Skilling. You know Claudia. Our star abroad.

Skilling   I believe I may have seen her in *Vogue*.

Roe   That was cropped from a profile in *Forbes*.

Lay   One of the fifty most powerful women, wasn't it?

Roe   I don't recall.

Skilling   Most powerful *women*?

Roe   Number fourteen.

Skilling   I remember. There was a great bit on Oprah and her dogs.

Roe   We were talking mark to market.

Skilling   I think one of her dogs was at number twelve.

Fastow   I just wanted to say congratulations – mark to market, much more appropriate, much more transparent. Exactly the right thing.

Skilling   Thanks. Are you –

Fastow   Sorry. Andy, Andy Fastow, you hired me –

Roe   This new accounting system, Jeff, you think it's worth celebrating?

Skilling   Well don't you?

Roe   I'm not an accountant.

Lay   You settled for fourteenth most powerful woman in the world.

Fastow   Mark to market is the accounting system for all the big investment banks / on Wall Street.

Roe   Yes. But *we* are a gas and oil company.

Fastow   No, you see –

Skilling   We're an *energy* company.

Lay (*gesturing to staff*)   I've been explaining mark to market, people get all tied up in knots.

Skilling   Seriously?

Lay   In what sense?

Skilling   There are people at this party who don't understand *the idea*?

Fastow   Mark to market lets us show the future / profits / –

Lay   / We know.

Skilling   / I know.

Skilling   My people have worked their asses off to get the SEC to understand and approve this –

Roe   And it's very much appreciated.

Skilling   Everyone gets mark to market here, right?

Fastow *exhales and glances at the group of* **Employees** *who had teased him.*

Fastow   I've talked to some people, I don't know …

Skilling   I've got slides I can bring down.

Roe   No.

Skilling   It doesn't kill you? Everyone standing around celebrating their ignorance –

Roe   It's not a celebration of ignorance, Jeff, it's a party.

Skilling   These people are getting *paid.*

Skilling *takes* **Fastow** *'s glass and clinks it to get everyone's attention. It's a surprise – any speech would be deemed to be* **Lay** *'s job.*

Skilling   Hi. Hi. Everybody. For those who don't know, I'm the reason you're here. I said I would only join this company if we started to use Mark to Market. What does that mean? Anybody? Well, it's a way for us to realize the profits we're *gonna* make *now.* If *you* have an idea, if you sign a deal, say that we're gonna provide someone with a supply of champagne for the next few years at a set price, every month whatever – Then that definite *future income* can be valued, at market prices today, and written down as *earnings* the moment the deal is signed. We don't have to wait for the grapes to be grown and squashed and … however the hell you make champagne.

The market will recognise your idea and your profit in that moment. And the company will pay you for it. If you come up with something brilliant – You know, life is so short. If you have a moment of genius, that will be rewarded now. No one should be able to kick back in your job years from now and take all the credit for the idea you had.

Fastow   They'll have to have their own ideas.

Skilling   Right. This guy gets it. Any questions? Anyone not understand? Okay, well. Have a party.

Skilling *turns and walks back to* **Lay,** **Roe** *and* **Fastow.**

Roe   Nicely done.

Skilling *downs his drink.*

Skilling   I should have brought the fucking slides.

We see projections of the joys and stability of the 1990s:

Bill Clinton, the break up of the Soviet Union, Microsoft, the Internet and the rise of the home computer and Intel, Friends, *Nelson Mandela's election, images of Arnie in* Terminator 2.

An **Employee** *comes forward to speak to us.*

Employee 3 (*to us*)   The nineties. It's a time of little conflict internationally, the fastest growing economy there *has ever been.* And the fashions are pretty good too. There's a new administration; a president who plays the saxophone. He's a Democrat but he understands the South.

It feels, genuinely, like the most exciting time to do business in the history of the world. There's a feeling that the people who are gonna change things aren't in parliaments or palaces, but in corporate boardrooms all over the United States of America.

Scene Two – Afterparty

In a corporate boardroom, high up, **Skilling** *and* **Roe** *finish having clothed, quick sex.*

Roe   I've been thinking about mark to market.

Skilling *laughs at her immediate switch to professionalism.*

Skilling   That's … concerning.

Skilling *is doing his pants up.* **Roe** *is pulling her skirt down and straightening herself.*

Roe   Essentially, we are deciding what our own future profits will be.

Skilling   No. The market is. You want to have this argument *now*?

Roe   All I said is we get to decide the profits. Why would that be anything but a good thing?

Skilling   Right. But you're wrong.

Roe   Spiky. Look at you! Look at your face!

Skilling   What?

Roe   You just changed is all.

I'll bet you *were* a real serious kid. My oldest is like that.

Skilling   Not … really.

Roe   You know, I read that it's better to hire people who were bullied at school. Cos they want it more. They've got in-built competition.

Skilling   I wasn't bullied! I got things quicker. When you get things quicker. You begin to resent people who don't.

Roe   You thought you were special.

Skilling   No, hey, I was drunk when I told you that stuff. I don't want to get on the couch about it.

Roe   Oooh! 'Whatever.'

Skilling   You know what, we accept that some people are prettier than other people and their lives are probably easier and we accept that some people are funnier – … But if you're smarter. You're supposed to walk around like you're shamed by it. Like everyone's viewpoint is equally valid. Well it's not, some people are fucking idiots.

Roe (*laughs*)   Not here.

Skilling   No, not here. Exactly.

They look out a window over Houston.

Skilling   I love a work place at night. No banality.

Roe   Before the market opens. The world waiting.

Beat.

Skilling (*to* **Roe**)   We need to talk about a thing.

Roe   Ohh(!) Ken told you.

Beat.

Skilling (*lying*)   Yeah.

Roe   Yeah. I like how you bring it up *after* you screwed me /

Skilling   / What did he say to *you*?

Roe   I'm not gonna break that confidence. But if you think when I'm president, you're getting special favours –

Skilling   Wait, Rich is leaving?!

Roe   No. Shit. Yes.

Skilling   You're getting *President*?!

Roe   You said you knew.

Skilling   No! /

Roe   You are a real son of a … I can't / believe –

Skilling   / I was gonna say Susan and I have separated.

Beat.

Roe   Oh my god!

Skilling   Rich is leaving Enron?

Roe   Do I need to feel guilty?

Skilling   Has Lay offered you the job?

Roe   I can't be the cause of a *marriage* break up –

Skilling   / I can't believe he's going.

Roe   We've only had sex three times.

Skilling   Rich is leaving(!) And it's four times.

Roe   Yes Rich is leaving. And I had sex with you three times.

Skilling   That is wrong but –

Roe   One, South America. Two, after the SEC announcement – three –

Skilling   / You forgot the plane.

Beat.

Roe   How are you defining sex?

Skilling   Sex. Penetration.

Roe   We did not have penetrative sex on the Enron jet! We fooled around. I went down on you.

Skilling   That's penetration! I was penetrating your –

Roe   Oh my god, well if you want to throw that in … (!)

Skilling   I don't want to throw anything in(!) – it doesn't matter, nothing will be penetrated anymore.

Roe   When did Susan leave?

Skilling   Has he offered you the job?

Roe   That's none of your business. When did your wife leave?

Skilling   *I* left. She *left*. But I – *left*.

Roe   I hope I'm irrelevant.

Skilling   You are entirely irrelevant.

Roe   Good.

Beat.

Skilling   Will I have to call you Madam President?

Roe   Come on, how old are you?!

Skilling   I'm forty-two.

Roe   Yeah.

Skilling   Oh god.

Roe   Stop it. You're Harvard, you're McKinsey, you're running a whole division. You're just having a mid-life / – (crisis)

Skilling   It's not that.

I've been thinking. Waking up at night with all these ideas. Ideas for here.

You know, maybe every extraordinary thing that's ever happened was conceived by a man alone in a room at four in the morning.

Roe   Oh, really? I think most acts of depravity too.

Look, don't get all … I'm sure you got ideas. I'll talk to Ken –

Skilling   He doesn't get me. I didn't grow up on a farm.

Roe *smiles.*

Roe   And you're a godless atheist.

Skilling   I'd like to be the other thing. Be nice.

Roe   It is nice.

She picks up her underwear and puts it in her handbag.

Roe   You gonna go home?

Skilling *shakes his head.*

Skilling   No. I'm going back to work.

She eyes him.

Roe   As an addendum, can I just say, previously you had an incentive equal, I believe, to mine for not disclosing this. I'd like to stress that this and the other three occasions, or four if you're gonna be a high school girl about it, are not to be discussed or recounted at any future date. And it will not happen again.

Skilling   Wow.

Roe   You got a Kleenex. I appear to be running.

Skilling *gets a tissue out of his pocket.* **Roe** *takes it and gently wipes all the way up her inner leg, wiping off the ejaculate that has run down her thigh.*

She tosses the Kleenex away deliberately casually and confidently strides from the office.

Scene Three – Ken Lay's Office – 1996

Bill Clinton (*on screen*)   I did not have sexual relations with that woman, Miss Lewinsky. I never told anybody to lie. Not a single time. Never.

News footage of the stories dominating American screens:

The OJ Simpson trial, Microsoft, supermodels, the divorce of Charles and Diana, and other distracting and comprehensible news items.

In another office, **Ken Lay** *sits with* **Roe** *and* **Skilling** *sat before him.*

Lay   What is Enron? In the past, folks thought that the basic unit of society would be the state, or the church or lord help us, the political party. But we now know it's The Company. And the family. And those two things should be the same. A place where a group of like-minded individuals work for the betterment of themselves and for those they love. I believe in God, I believe in democracy and I believe in the company. Now I think it's right for Rich to be leaving, I think it's the right decision. It does put me in the position of needing myself a president.

Skilling   Yes.

Roe   I imagine you'd want to indicate that Enron is not an old-fashioned, macho place to work.

Skilling   'Macho'. That's subtle.

Lay   Where is our company going?

Pause. **Lay** *leans back.*

The competitors look at each other. Dual dialogue.

Beat.

Roe   Ken, before he talks over me here I wanna say –

I don't know how aware you are of people's reputations but Jeff is not a people person –

He doesn't have the skills to manage people effectively –

Skilling   I want to build a trading floor –

A different sort of company. Hire the best graduates, if they're not top two per cent we don't want 'em. Make Wall Street look like Sesame Street.

Roe   He has trouble relating to others. He doesn't remember names. He called a client stupid.

Skilling   What client?

Roe   Fan Bridglen.

Skilling   I have no idea who that is.

Roe *makes a 'see?' gesture.*

Skilling   You're a politician, Claud. I've never claimed to be.

Lay   Some of my best friends are politicians.

You wanna build a trading floor?

Skilling   Yes sir.

Lay   For trading?

Skilling   Ask me what I want to trade.

Lay   What were *you* gonna say, Claudia?

Roe   My vision. *The* international energy company. Enron: delivering gas and oil to the world.

Skilling (*spits it*)   That's a parochial vision.

Roe   *The world* is?

Jeff, sometimes I wonder if you have anger issues.

Skilling   Fuck you.

Beat.

Ask me. What. I would trade.

Lay   What do you see us trading, Jeff?

Skilling   Energy.

Roe   Brilliant(!)

Skilling   Sure, we make it. We transport it. We sell it. Why don't we *trade* it? You gotta pull back and look at this thing from above. Why do we even have to deliver the gas at all?

Roe   We're a gas company, Jeff.

Skilling (*to* **Lay**)   If we got a customer wants a steady supply of natural gas and we don't have a pipeline near them, what do we do?

Lay   We buy the gas from someone who does have a pipeline there and we charge the customer a little more than we paid for it.

Skilling   So let's always do that. Buy from someone, sell it on. In. Out. Without ever having to deliver the gas or maintain the pipeline. We can send energy through the air in nothing but numbers.

Roe   We should be focusing on building more plants.

Skilling   God, if you could hear yourself. 'Build more fucking powerplants'. No imagination, go crazy – What about wind farms or hydro –!?

Roe   *Wind farms*?! I'm sorry I though I was the only woman in the room.

Skilling   We don't need the hard stuff.

Roe   India, Africa – huge power requirements in the future –

Skilling   That will take *years*! You really want to pay for people to go build pipelines along disputed borders, tribes with AK47s. You want that fucking *mess* –?

Roe   I think in the most volatile areas in the world it might be worth controlling their energy supply, yes.

Skilling   Scratching around in the dirt. I'm not talking about pushing on an industry already in place. I'm trying to tell you … Ken, you've seen some changes in business since you started.

Lay   Sure. I'm as old as the plains.

Skilling   Well it's time to evolve again. We *have to. America doesn't have the natural resources anymore*. Not really. And that's good, that's fine. We have intellectual capital and the best of it in the world. Look at the societies that *do* have the raw materials, how modern do they feel, really? Then take a landlocked, barren country like Switzerland. What do they do? They invent *banking*.

We should be coming up with new ideas. About everything. Employ the smartest people we can find. Have 'em free to look at whatever they want – less structure, less routine, let people's minds work, free from the old assumptions about what this company is.

Roe   Sounds like hippy talk to me.

Skilling   I'm not gonna patronize you by pretending you believe what you just said.

Lay   You've got one idea about trading.

Skilling   I got plenty of ideas. Mark to market, energy trading, that's just the beginning.

Roe   I can push through natural gas deals we already have experience of. All over the world. You want power? Enron. India? Enron. South America? Enron.

Skilling   Countries are meaningless.

It's all going to be virtual. Oil and land run out.

Roe   In which case, don't you think it's worth being the only people in the world with power plants?!

Skilling   There's a whole, glistening, clean industry above what you're talking about that no one's even thought of yet.

Roe   Except you(!)

Silence. **Lay** *leans back.*

Lay   You see, I'm like Claudia. I like holding things – you know. In our daddy's day, a man worked and he saw himself in his work. If he made a table, he saw himself in the table he made. It was part of him, and he of it. I *am* oil and pipelines.

Skilling   My father was a valve salesman. I didn't want to grow up to sell valves. Tiny pieces of something bigger he never saw. There is a dignity to holding something, Ken. But your daddy was a Baptist preacher. There's a dignity to giving people something they *can't* touch.

Roe   Suddenly you have a 'calling'. Well, I find it distasteful.

Skilling   I don't want to work for you. I feel I gotta say if Claudia takes this job I won't be staying.

Lay *considers the younger man and his presumption.*

Lay (*to* **Skilling**)   I think you should step out.

Skilling *tries to maintain his dignity and leaves.* **Lay** *takes* **Roe**'s *hand.*

Lay (*to* **Roe**)   You know, you were always my favourite. But I'm offering Jeff the job.

*As **Roe**'s dreams are shattered, **Skilling**'s dreams are made real.*

*The transformation of Enron. From discrete, regular offices, **Skilling** and **Lay** oversee it becoming an open-plan, free, shiny expanse.*

It should feel like a physical liberation; a clearing of clutter.

Lay (*to us*)   Henry Ford. There's a man folks think revolutionized things. He did not. He took people out of the equation. Of which I do not approve. No, the man who ought to be remembered is Alfred P. Sloane – Head of General Motors and a great philanthropist. There was a time when the cost of the automobile meant that most Americans could never afford one. And General Motors felt there must be a way to open up that market. Over at Ford, Henry didn't care. Ford felt that only a man who'd saved every single cent for a car deserved one. And if he had not the money, he should not have the car. Never mind that meant the automobile was only available to the very rich. Now Alfred P. Sloane said, well hang on a minute, if a man will pledge to pay the full amount of the car in installments, over time, we will provide him with one. And when we do, he will use that car to travel to a place of work, where he will make more money than he might otherwise, thus he will use that very car in his effort to make good on his promise. And in such a way the common man was given access to the automobile. And in such a way General Motors overtook Ford as the most successful and profitable company in America. And in such a way, the world was changed.

Today I am pleased to announce the appointment of Jeffrey Skilling to the post of President of the Enron corporation.

They shake hands.

Skilling *looks down at the Enron he envisioned beneath him; glass, reflective surfaces, futuristic design, open spaces, a huge trading floor.*

Scene Four – An Orgy of Speculation

Skilling   Let's trade.

Magical music.

Above us somewhere, there is a twinkle of gold. And then another of silver somewhere else. And then more, commodities like stars in the sky.

The sound of singing, each their own different song. It builds to an atonal babble of commodity prices and bids. It's a musical cacophony of the trading floor. Over time, the voices all conjoin to meet at a pure, single note. It is beautiful.

Voices (*sung*)   Gold. Up twenty-five.

The gold glints somewhere in the auditorium.

The voices and notes become an atonal mess again. Eventually blending to everyone singing a single note and price.

Voices (*sung*)   Aluminium. Down one.

A shimmer from aluminium.

And again the clamor builds up before finding a commodity value in one distinct harmony.

Voices (*sung*)   Natural gas. Up five seventy-one.

Voices   Orange juice. Down fourteen.

They split again into babble.

Voices   Pork belly. Up seven twenty-four.

This empty, beautiful purity in **Skilling**'s *head is interrupted by the reality of the* **Traders**' *arrival.*

The **Traders** *flood the stage. The stock price rises.*

The chaos, the physicality, the aggression and shouting of a trading floor. This simmers to doing deals, buzzing, on phones and computers making money. Overlap is fine.

A melee of sound and trading and speculation into –

Trader 5   I'm waiting on a call from Louisiana. Are you in play?

Trader 3   Speculation confirmed.

Trader 6   Spread's widened.

Trader 3   Another bid. What's the market doing?

Trader 5   What's the market doing?

Trader 7   Crude is up.

Trader 5   Gimme price.

Trader 7   Twenty-three.

Trader 1   Yes!

Trader 4   If market closes below twenty-one, this guy's fucked

Trader 1   I really am.

Trader 1   I lose a million.

Trader 6   Hey, it's *at* twenty-three –

Trader 2   *For now* …

Trader 7   Dropping!

Trader 1   Oh fuck. I'm gonna lose a million dollars. Fuck.

Trader 3   Hey, market's not closed yet.

Trader 5   There goes your bonus.

Trader 1   Bonus ain't shit. I just don't want Jeff Skilling up my ass.

Trader 6   Chill, dude. Skilling gets it. He's a fucking trader, man.

Trader 3   You've drunk the Kool-Aid.

Trader 5   Tell him about last week.

Trader 6   Oh yeah. You were in Dallas.

Trader 4   Is this the shit with me?

Trader 6   Look at this kid, twenty-six years old – hey, you tell it.

Trader 4   So I had a big loss.

Trader 1   How much?

Trader 4   I got down twenty million / dollars.

Trader 6   Twenty million.

Trader 4   In one day.

Trader 5 *whistles the loss.*

Trader 4   It's not a good day.

Trader 5   And it's the day Jeff's coming down to visit the floor.

Trader 2   He's pacing and crying around the place.

Trader 4   It was twenty million dollars!

Trader 2   'It was twenty million dollars!'

Trader 5   Any Wall Street Bank'd push him off the roof then check his teeth for gold.

Trader 2   We thought it was hilarious.

Trader 4   You did, I remember that.

Trader 6   And Skilling's heard about the loss.

Trader 2   Sure he has.

Trader 4   There's nothing Skilling don't know. And he comes in, he makes a bee line for my desk and everybody watches.

Trader 2   He goes over and he puts his arm round this fuck, and he says, what does he say?

Trader 4   He says, 'Only people prepared to lose are ever gonna win.' And he slaps me on the back and he leaves.

Trader 5   Slaps him on the back.

Trader 4   And he leaves!

Trader 2   True story.

Trader 4   And that's Jeffrey fucking Skilling.

Trader 2   Hey, anyone invited to Mexico here?

Trader 5   For what?

Trader 2   One of Skilling's death weekends, man! Rolling jeeps and motorcycles and wotnot. Someone's gonna fuckin die /

Trader 5   That is the coolest thing.

Trader 2   And Fastow gets to go. Lapdog motherfucker.

Trader 7   Going up!

Trader 4   You seen that double breasted douchebag? Thinks he's Sinatra.

Trader 2   What the fuck Skilling see in the guy?

Trader 3   We're going into electricity, a whole new market and you get Fastow to run it, I mean, really, *Fastow*?

Suddenly, **Fastow** *enters, all smooth self-importance. All the* **Traders** *react mockingly.*

Trader 5   Oh jeez, here it is.

Fastow   Yeah, hi. You gotta help with some figures. The electricity retail market.

Trader 3   You're kidding right? We're closing deals here.

Fastow   I'm here on behalf of Jeffrey Skilling.

One of the **Traders** *makes a 'whoo' noise.*

Trader 2   We don't have shit on your retail markets. We're traders.

Fastow   Just get me whatever numbers you've got on electricity suppliers you trade with, that's your fucking job.

Trader 2   No, that's your fucking job and you're asking me to do it.

Skilling gets that, right?

Fastow *goes for* **Trader 2**, *physically. He gets right in his face, aggressively.*

Trader 5   Crude down six.

Trader 1   Fuck, man!

Fastow   I don't have time for you to be whoever the fuck you are!

Trader 2   Is this guy serious?

Fastow *touches him.*

Fastow   I'm very serious.

Trader 3   Whoa whoa whoa.

Trader 2   Get your fucking hands off me.

Trader 2 *shoves* **Fastow.** **Fastow** *falls to the floor. Pandemonium.*

Trader 3   Come on, Fastow, you'll get destroyed.

Trader 3 *moves in to break it up.*

Fastow *is pulled away.*

Trader 1   Oh god, crude's falling.

Trader 5   You're gonna take it in the ass.

Fastow   I want that recorded!

Trader 3   I gotta fine you for that.

Trader 2   Fuck, Clem.

Trader 3   That was physical on the floor.

Trader 2   But it's Fastow!

Trader 3   I gotta take two hundred.

Fastow *watches, pleased.* **Trader 2** *reaches into his pockets and doles out a whole heap of bills on the floor.*

Trader 2   Take *five* hundred. Cos I'm gonna fucking finish.

Trader 2 *swings around and goes for* **Fastow,** *who, not expecting this, scrambles out of the way to the other side of the space. Other* **Traders** *mock and physically berate him. One shows him his penis.*

Fastow   (That's illegal.)

As **Fastow** *beats a hasty retreat he tries to maintain some dignity.*

Fastow   I'll remember that when I'm CFO.

Fastow *exits.*

Trader 2   Did everybody see that?

Trader 4   Big hat no cattle, muthafucka.

Trader 3 (*genuinely staggered*)   Is it me or did that guy just come in here and say, tell me how to sell electricity?

Trader 5   I think he did.

Trader 3   Unbelievable. Hey, market closing!

The bell rings for end of trading.

Trader 1   This is it, this is it!

Trader 4   What's the price?

Trader 5   Someone call it!

Improvisation of trading at its highest pitch.

Market closes.

Trader 4   Boom!

Trader 1   COME ON!

Trader 1 *is delighted, sweating, filled with testosterone and joy.*

Trader 4   You're one lucky fucking cock-sucking cash-loving son of a bitch!

Cheers.

Trader 1 (*to us*)   I wish you knew. You're right, you were right, it's there in a number, right in front of you and no one can dispute it. This is the purest place to work in the world. You know where you come if you're top of your class? Here. You know where Wall Street wishes it was? Here. We don't just play the game, we are the game. There's you and the guy on the other end of the deal, and who can move faster and who can move smarter. But it's not just up here. There's something … primal. Closest thing there is to hunting. Closest thing there is to sex. For a man, that is.

Lights of commodity prices over the faces of all the traders, a sea of figures.

Alan Greenspan (*on screen*)   (Clearly, sustained low inflation implies *less uncertainty* about the future, and lower risk premiums imply *higher prices of stocks and other earning* assets. But how do we know when *irrational exuberance* has unduly escalated asset values …) irrational exuberance … irrational exuberance …

Scene Five – Trimming the Fat

The sound of motorbikes revving, screeching brakes, the hum of manly pursuits.

Split scene.

Below:

Enron gym.

Skilling *is on a running machine, in sports clothes. He's pushing himself and relishing the physical challenge.*

Above:

Ken Lay'*s office.* **Lay** *and* **Roe** *are meeting.*

Below:

Fastow *enters the gym with trepidation in a suit.*

Skilling   Andy Fastow.

Fastow   You want me to go wait somewhere?

Skilling   This is the meeting. Get on.

Skilling *gestures to running machine beside him.*

Fastow*, nervous, takes off his shoes and jacket and gets on the machine.*

Skilling *immediately ups it to a run for* **Fastow**.

Fastow   I'm sorry I screwed up Electricity.

Skilling   Yeah you have. You know I was supposed to announce it on the tour today?

Fastow   Yeah. I tried, I really –

Skilling   I heard you got aggravated on some trader?

Fastow   I –

Skilling   They'll do that to ya.

Fastow   I won't be mocked.

Skilling   Is that right?

Skilling *can't help smiling a little. He ups* **Fastow***'s speed, along with his own.* **Fastow** *tries to keep up.*

Skilling   You ever read those business books, how to win friends and … the seven secrets of highly effective people and stuff like that –

Fastow   Yeah, I –

Skilling   Don't. It's bullshit. Read Dawkins, *The Selfish Gene*?

Fastow   I don't know it –

Skilling   Guy named Richard Dawkins. Read Darwin.

Fastow   Am I getting fired, Jeff?

Skilling   By rights you should be out. I got this company running on Darwinian principles.

Skilling *ups* **Fastow***'s speed again.*

Fastow *redoubles his efforts.*

Fastow   Please don't fire me!

Skilling   Charles Darwin showed how an idea can change the world. Now we understand our own nature. And we can use that.

Fastow   Use it for what?

Skilling   For business. Business *is* nature.

Fastow   Like self-interest and competition?

Skilling   Exactly. Money and sex motivate people, Andy. And money's the one that gets their hands off their dick and into work.

Above:

Roe   I don't know if I can work under this regime, Ken.

Lay   Come on now, Claudia.

Roe   I mean it.

Lay   I don't like this fighting. This is a family!

Roe   Well families fight! And Jeff doesn't listen to anyone.

Lay   He could learn something from you in charm, I'll give you that.

Roe   How am I supposed to run a division where ten per cent of my people are cut every time we have an evaluation?!

Lay   It's the bottom ten per cent.

Roe   Who don't get replaced! Or they get replaced with really smart twenty-year-olds with no idea what's going on!

Lay   It's a strategy! Gimme a break, Claudia, you gotta be nice to me today. It's my birthday.

Roe   It is? Well, happy birthday, Ken.

Lay   Fact I got a card from an old friend's son.

Lay *passes it to* **Roe**.

Roe   'Happy birthday, Kenny Boy! Now you're really old! Call me sometime. From *W.*'

Lay   He ain't got the manners of his daddy. But I think we got a shot at the White House with him. Stick around, it's gonna get interesting.

Below:

Skilling   Run you fucker!

Fastow I'm gonna have a heart attack.

Skilling That's cos you're weak.

Fastow I'm sorry I fucked up Electricity!

Skilling What did you say?

Fastow I'm sorry I fucked up Electricity!

Skilling I can't hear you!

Fastow I'm sorry!

Skilling *presses the stop button on* **Fastow**'s *running machine, hurling the younger man from his treadmill.*

As **Fastow** *regains his balance and composure as* **Skilling** *calmly slows his own speed.*

Skilling Never apologize, Andy.

Skilling *gets off his machine.*

Skilling Fact is, it's not all your fault.

An exhausted **Fastow** *agrees physically while he pants.*

Skilling Electricity's an industry with no competition, no natural selection. The fact is retail is never gonna make money until electricity gets deregulated.

Fastow Yes! Deregulate electricity and that market's ours.

Skilling That's what I'm looking for. It's a political decision though. Ken's dealing with it.

Fastow That's great. So I can keep my job?

Beat.

Skilling Are you smart, Andy?

Fastow Yeah, I am.

Skilling I'm fucking smart. And I like guys with spikes. I didn't know you had any til I heard about you taking on a pack of traders.

Now that takes a special kind of stupid. But also balls. You started in finance?

Fastow   Yeah.

Skilling   Let's get you back there. I know your background, you're an abstracts man. Securitization. Risk assessment. I never met anyone less suited to retail in my life. Let's get you down in finance. Where you can keep away from people.

Fastow   Thank you. Yeah! I won't let you down!

Above:

Lay   What is it you want?

Roe   I want to build a power plant in India.

Lay   India? Nobody's in India.

Roe   You wanna be the first? Jeff won't go for it, he doesn't even think outside the States. One power plant.

Lay   'One power plant!'

Roe   It's India, Ken. The size of it. Don't you want some skin in that game?

Beat.

Lay   Okay, let's get into your power plant.

Roe   I knew I could come to you.

Lay   I understand your concerns about Jeff. But look, we got the stock analysts coming in today to rate the company. Let's see what Jeff Skilling means for the share price.

As **Lay** *says 'share price' the share price is revealed; a figurative representation of the company's worth, represented by light somewhere on stage.*

An **Analyst** *enters and speaks to us.*

Sloman (*to us*)   An analyst rates a company's stock to the outside world. We're go-betweens. The first port of call for someone looking to invest their money. Where's safe? Where's profitable? We'll rate a company at 'Buy', 'Sell' or 'Hold'. Why trust what we think? Well. We know the world, we're from the world. We're employed by the biggest investment banks and brokerage firms so we know how it works. You need access to hear the rumours, to get the skinny. It takes years to get access, to build up knowledge. A company needs customers and good press maybe, but if it really wants to thrive? It's us they need to impress.

The **Analysts** *are* **Sheryl Sloman** *of Citigroup,* **JP Morgan** *and* **Deutsche Bank**. *All follow* **Skilling**, *enraptured.*

As he walks around the space, various employees approach **Skilling** *with contracts for him to approve and sign. He smoothly signs though barely looks at them, treating them like autographs.*

Skilling   Ladies and Gentlemen, Enron is a new kind of company. You want to see the next big thing? It's in the minds of one of these people. We're not just an energy company, we're a powerhouse for ideas. No other company lets people work as freely and creatively as we do. If you hire only the most brilliant people you can create new industries, new economies and reinvent the old ones. The league we're in? We're not the Houston Oilers, we're not even the Dallas Cowboys. We're the whole damn NFL.

The **Analysts** *line up and face the audience.*

Skilling   Now, let's see Citigroup!

The **Citigroup Analyst**, *after a drum roll, reveals his/her verdict*

Citigroup Analyst   Strong buy!

The stock goes up.

Skilling   And JP Morgan!

JP Morgan Analyst   Strong buy!

The stock goes up.

Skilling   And finally … Deutsche Bank!

Deutsche Bank (*in German*)   … Strong buy!

The stock goes up.

It's reached half of its full height. **Skilling** *looks genuinely touched by this.*

The **Analysts** *become a barber shop quartet and sing:*

Analysts (*singing*)

ENRON, ENRON, ENRON, ENRON.
If your company bank accounts need filling!
He's available, and willing.
To see to it that you make a killing!
Skilling, Skilling, Skilling, Skilling, Skilling,
Be boo doo wop wop ba doo!

Skilling   Thank you for recognizing our work and I'm happy –

Skilling *notices the stock price rise.*

Skilling   I'm so excited –

He sees it rise again.

Skilling   I'm a little sad?

It drops very slightly.

Skilling   Ha! I'm Enron.

He's delighted by his power and effect. Grinning at the recognition and level of belief.

Lay *comes down and approaches his protégé.*

Lay   I got something for you, golden boy.

Lay *hands him a fifty-dollar bill.*

Skilling   What, are you tipping me, Ken?

Lay   I'm handing out fifty-dollar bills to every employee I see today. My own money. This is the first time we've hit a fifty-dollar share price!

Skilling   Is it right you're taking the jet later?

Lay   Yeah. Going to visit the kids.

Skilling   The *company* jet?

Lay   Time with the family. That's important.

Skilling   Just thought we were getting you out to Washington?

Lay   I'm stopping off in Washington. Bill and I are playing a little golf. I'll pretend I don't see him switching the balls in the rough.

Skilling   But deregulation's on that agenda?

Lay   Relax, will ya? These things take time.

Skilling   Okay, well, enjoy your kids.

Scene Six – Time is Money

A memory.

Daughter (*V.O.*)   One, two, three, four, five, six … seven, six …

Skilling   You can do this. Seven …

Skilling's Daughter   *appears somewhere high up, not close to him.*

Daughter   Show me the money!

Skilling (*amused*)   God, I can't believe your mother let you watch that.

Daughter   Show me the money!

Skilling   Okay, once more, but you count with me this time.

Skilling *gets a stack of one-dollar bills out of his pocket and begins counting them out ostentatiously, as a familiar game.*

Skilling   One, two, three, four, five, six, seven … come on! / Seven …

Daughter   / Seven, eight, nine, ten!

Skilling   Good girl. Eleven, twelve … How long you think before I've counted out a million dollars?

Daughter   Um.

She doesn't know, she fidgets.

Skilling   One dollar bill a second. No stopping, how long before I counted out a million dollars? – Guess.

She makes a noise, enjoying the attention of her dad but not comprehending.

Skilling   It would take Daddy at one dollar a second, eleven days to count out a million dollars. Eleven days! No sleeping.

Daughter   Again!

Skilling   What d'you mean again? Okay, one, two, three, four … how long would it take for Daddy to count out a *billion* dollars!

Daughter   No!

Skilling   Yeah there's such a thing, a *billion* dollars! One, two, three, four – I'm gonna do it now –

Daughter   No!

Skilling   Okay. I'll work it out instead.

He calculates in his head.

Skilling   Counting a billion dollars would take me … thirty-two years?!

He scowls, checks.

Skilling   Yeah, around thirty-two years.

*His **Daughter** fades into the dark.*

Daughter (*V.O.*)   One, two, three, four, five, six, seven …

The counting continues into:

Skilling   Okay people! Come on! Time is money!

Physical sequence:

The company at work. The **Traders** *dance. As they do they create a round table.* **Skilling** *holds meetings around it. People come and go. Meetings end and begin. Fast, ordered, fluidity. Numbers fly through the air. The stock price throbs, but never altering much, gradually edging up in comforting, rhythmic pulses. Time passes.*

Eventually, **Claudia Roe** *makes her way through the building to* **Skilling**'s *office.*

Scene Seven – Skilling's Office

Skilling *is watching the financial news.*

Roe   I've been trying to avoid you.

Skilling   Well. This is my office.

Roe   Yeah. Maybe it was the wrong place to come.

Skilling *turns the sound down on the television.*

Skilling   You probably want Ken's office. It's just down the hall.

Roe   Come on.

Skilling   Have you seen the stock price today?

Roe   I see it every day. I see in the elevator, I see it on the walls. I see it on my desk.

He nods.

Roe   I said to people, wait, just wait, the shine'll wear off, get ready for the dip folks. And … . a year goes by, two. But I keep saying it because, if I stop, it's bound to happen and the worst thing would be to not being able to say I told you so.

Skilling   Well. I'm sure you've got more class than that.

Roe   I don't. I don't think you do either. Go on, you can say it.

Skilling   It's not about that.

Roe   Oh come on! I know what you guys call my division on your biking weekends in Mexico.

Skilling   That's traders. I don't call it that.

Roe   Tits Industries. It's not even clever. At least it used to be … what did it used to be?

Skilling   I don't know.

Roe   You know.

Skilling   Skank of America.

She nods. Beat.

Roe   I came by to say an old college friend of mine emailed. He's a professor at Harvard now. He used to drink his own urine for a dare by the way. Now he's a professor. Anyways. He asked if I could put him in touch with you. They want to use Enron as one of the business models they teach.

Skilling   At Harvard?

Roe   Yeah.

Skilling   Give him my number.

Roe   I did. Just don't ask him for the stories about *me.*

Skilling   I heard about your party for the opening of the plant at Dabhol.

Roe   It was a great party.

Skilling   You hired an elephant.

Roe   Shame you couldn't make it.

Skilling   I don't have time to jet off to your consolation prize in India. I'm running a company here.

Roe   Ouch.

Beat.

Skilling   You know the whole thing was a coward's way of getting things done.

Roe   I had to go to Ken. You wouldn't have – Every time I look at my assets there's less of 'em. You're selling everything I have!

Skilling   That's not true.

Roe   It is! I'm running a division which isn't expanding, it's not even contracting, it's having its *balls* cut off.

Skilling   That's business!

Roe   It's *your* business.

Skilling   Damn right it is!

Roe   I'm fighting to survive here!

Skilling   Either I'm running this company or Ken is.

Roe   You should tell *him* that.

Skilling   I do! He just … nods and … gives me a cigar!

Roe   It's his company.

Skilling   It's the shareholders' company.

Beat.

Roe   You need smart people around. To disagree with you.

Skilling   I don't know if Ken is the smartest guy ever to run a company or the dumbest motherfucker in the world.

Roe   I meant me. You look good, by the way.

Skilling   I … you mean I lost weight.

Roe   Sure, but. You know three guys in my division got Lasex on their eyes after you. Can't find a soul in the building with glasses now. Everyone's copying Daddy.

Skilling   It works.

Roe   It's not dangerous?

Skilling   Well, I don't know, Claud, I guess. It's lasers in your eyes.

She uses this as an excuse to look into his eyes.

She's deliberately close to his face. She puts her hands on his face.

Roe   Have you ever failed at anything, Jeffrey Skilling?

Beat.

Skilling   Don't. I don't think that's / (a very good idea)

Roe   / I'm not.

Beat. **Skilling** *closes his eyes. He leans in.*

Just then, over her shoulder, **Skilling** *spots a massive graphic flash up on the screen showing the financial news – 'ENRON!'*

Skilling *spins around. Once he sees what she's referring to, he's just as excited as* **Roe***.*

They both scrabble for the volume control. One gets there first and turns it up.

Business Anchor – Gayle   Welcome back, I'm Gayle Davenport.

Analyst – Elise   And I am Elise Deluka.

Business Anchor – Gayle   (By close of market today, energy darling Enron's stock rose 26 per cent in a single day to a new high of $67.25. That's staggering isn't it, Elise?)

Analyst – Elise   (It sure is, Gayle. That's why we're naming them our Must Buy of the Week!)

Business Anchor – Gayle   (It's astounding their ambition and creativity –)

Analyst – Elise   (Yeah, yeah – they're unstoppable. They're the light of the new economy. I mean, I'd rate them, right now, at being worth sixty billion dollars.)

Business Anchor – Gayle   So Jeffrey Skilling over / at Enron's certainly doing something right! /

Analyst – Elise   / He sure is!

Skilling *reacts to his name.*

Business Anchor – Gayle   (Now let's go over to Francine for a tale of two very different cities …)

Roe   Sixty billion dollars! How can we be worth sixty billion dollars?!

Skilling   If someone's prepared to pay that much then that's what we're worth –

Roe   But that's huge! That's fantastic!

Skilling   Sixty billion dollars. That's nearly two thousand years.

Beat.

Roe   What?

Skilling   Forget it.

Fuck. How is that possible?!

Roe   Hey, we're announcing profits all the time. Everyone's behind you! And I'm just saying that includes me.

Skilling   Yeah.

She makes to leave.

Roe   Oh, and I don't know if you heard. You know your guy in finance, with the suit and the hair?

Skilling   Andy Fastow?

Roe   He's had a baby. Little boy. Named him Jeffrey.

Scene Eight – An Unholy Partnership

Below, darkly, **Fastow**'s *lair; a dingy place at the bottom of Enron.* **Fastow** *flits happily between complex piles of paperwork, records and maybe screens.*

Fastow (*to us*)   I don't know if you're big fans of hedging. I can't see how you wouldn't be. A hedge is just a way of protecting yourself from risk. You literally hedge your bets. If you got a lot of money in airlines, for example. You might think, hey this is all going really well, lots of people fly – my investment is safe and going up. But what happens if there's a huge airplane crash, maybe people die, oh no, folks get scared of flying and your stocks plunge. Well, the smart guy hedges his airline investment with – maybe – an investment in a car rental company. When air travel frightens people, they want to feel in control, they'll drive interstate. So when your airline shares go (*noise and motion of plane crashing*), your car rental shares go (*noise and motion of car brooming upwards*). So you never lose money. With enough imagination you don't ever have to lose anything. When I write down everything that can possibly go wrong, as a formula. A formula I control. Nothing seems scary anymore.

Fastow *goes back to his calculations.*

Skilling *enters.*

Skilling   Andy. Andy, you had a baby.

Fastow (*delighted*)   Yeah.

Skilling   Congratulations, fella. You got a picture?

Fastow   In my wallet.

Skilling   Okay.

Fastow *starts looking for his wallet.*

Fastow   Oh man, it's down the hall. Shall I –? You really wanna –

Skilling   I don't (mind). Do it next time.

Beat.

Fastow   He's called Jeffrey.

Skilling   Wow. Great name(!)

Fastow   Hey, who's done more for me in this world, you know?

Beat.

Skilling   You know what I was doing when my daughter was born?

Fastow   What?

Skilling   I was on the phone from the hospital negotiating my deal.
To come work here.

Pause.

Fastow   You get a good deal?

Skilling *makes a so-so gesture and sound.*

Fastow   You know when you have a baby and it gets handed to you
for the first time? I had this incredible, indescribable feeling; this
defining realization that in my life, from this point on – So. Many.
Things could go. Wrong.

Skilling   I guess.

Fastow   And I say that as a man who knows how to manage risk.
It's just the fear of losing something. Risk is life basically.

Beat.

Skilling   These. What are these?

Skilling *goes back to the piles of papers, he has found a few scraps
of papers, covered in complex scrawlings. Maybe half-screwed up.*

Fastow (*proud*)   Oh, these are the Raptors.

Skilling   Raptors?

Fastow   Financial models I'm / working –

Skilling   / Are these hedges?

Fastow   Not as you'd normally understand them. But they're a
way of managing risk. I'm playing with them. Just in my own time,
just for …

Skilling   For fun?!

Fastow (*finds all three*)   Raptor one, raptor two, raptor three …

Skilling   Raptors.

Fastow   *Jurassic Park.*

Skilling   You're thirty-seven years old.

Fastow   It's actually really well done.

Skilling   So these are protecting you against losses in investments.

Fastow   Yeah. Like, you know, with hedging how – say you got a lot of money in airlines –

Skilling   I know about your planes and cars thing, Andy, I've heard you at parties.

Fastow   Okay, well, I've been seeing if there's a way of making a model that acts like the car rental company, without actually having to actually give my money to the car rental company.

Casually intrigued, **Skilling** *looks through them all.*

Skilling   A little theoretical.

Fastow   Well, that's the thing. A theoretical car rental company hedges your airline investment just as good as a real one does. On the books.

Skilling   Well sure, unless planes fall.

Fastow   Yeah but they almost certainly won't. It's crazy to have all this money flying out the door for things that probably won't happen. This model locks in the high value of your first investment. You own that, that's real.

Skilling   These are interesting.

Fastow   Yeah …?

Skilling   I could do with more guys like you.

Fastow *beams.*

Skilling *is having some pain.*

Fastow   You okay?

Skilling   These shoes … they're not broken in.

Fastow   What size are you? You want mine?

Skilling   No, Andy, I don't want your shoes. Thanks.

Fastow   You like 'em? They're Italian.

Skilling   Yeah I, jeez, I don't know. They're fucking shoes.

Pause.

Fastow   Great news about the stock price.

Nothing.

Skilling   You want to get a beer?

Fastow (*excited*)   I got a beer.

Fastow *opens up a tiny fridge that's been installed somewhere in his office/lair.*

Skilling   You got a refrigerator?

Fastow   Yeah, I just asked 'em. I called up and said. Came down same day. Put it in.

Skilling   Who did?

Fastow   We did.

Skilling   Wow.

Fastow   It's a long way up to the … thing.

They open and drink two beers.

Skilling   I got a problem, Andy. We got great stock price. We're declaring huge profits using mark to market. Correctly. But those *actual* profits aren't coming in yet. So.

Fastow   There's losses.

Skilling   That's right. We've got the best business plan, the highest share price, the smartest graduates. Trouble is. Right now. We're not making any money.

Long pause.

Fastow   How bad?

Skilling   You with me?

Fastow   Always.

Skilling   I can't find. Any area. Right now. Except trading. And there, day to day, we might lose as much as we make.

Pause.

Fastow   Wow(!)

Skilling   Yeah(!)

Fastow   You're not kidding?

Skilling   I am not kidding.

I don't know what I'm gonna do. I don't mind taking losses. But I can't *report* taking losses right now. The gap between the perception and the reality is … (*he has one hand up at neck level indicating the high perception and the other he puts lower to indicate the reality.*)

Skilling *stares at him, holding his pose.*

Skilling   I don't know what I'm going to do.

His arms droop despondently. **Fastow** *dives in to hold the perception hand up.*

Fastow   Wait, you got a perception here, a reality here. You just need something for this to lean on while we bring this up.

Fastow *brings the lower hand up to meet the higher hand. Beat.* **Skilling** *shakes off the foolish physical intimacy.*

Skilling   If those Washington fucks would just deregulate electricity like Clinton promised, we'd *have* those profits!

Fastow   Hey. Fuck it. Two guys in a room.

You want my help?

Beat.

Skilling   What you got?

Fastow   How you doing with a Chief Financial Officer?

Skilling   I haven't found him yet.

Fastow   You considered everybody?

Skilling   Everybody / with experience (of) –

Fastow   / You considered me?

Skilling   For CFO …? One of the most powerful positions in / any corporation …?

Fastow   / Yeah.

Skilling   You're not a people person, Andy.

Fastow   You really care about that, Jeff?

Beat.

Skilling   Two guys in a room.

Fastow   You ever had an affair? When you were married.

Skilling   None of your fucking business.

Fastow   That's a yes.

Skilling   Is this something you've heard?

Fastow   No, okay, wait, that's wrong. You like porn?

Skilling   Do I –? I don't have time to take a *shit* –

Fastow   I think porn could save every marriage in this country. As internet porn goes up, divorce rates gonna go way down –

Fastow *makes gesture of one thing going up as the other goes down.*

Fastow   (That's the industry to get into, I'll say that …)

Skilling   Find the point.

Fastow   I want to give Enron a mistress.

Beat.

Skilling   That's why I like you, Andy. You're fucking nuts.

Fastow   Having something off the books, even if it's Jenna Jameson in an unmarked folder, your *virtual* mistress – she supports your marriage, strengthens it. We can do the same for a company.

Skilling   Explain.

Fastow   For those occasions we need to … 'offload'. We create a company that exists purely to fulfil Enron's needs.

Skilling   Example.

Fastow   We could push debt, we could push those losses into this other entity, *sell it* to this entity. So we make money *and* move a loss off the books, wait for it to turn to profit –

Skilling   Then move it back.

Why doesn't everyone do this?

Fastow   How would we know if they did?

Skilling   Andy.

Fastow   I mean it! This is an area where we're expected to be creative. The regulations *encourage* it.

Skilling   This isn't one of your theoretical models. A whole investment fund with money enough to buy bad assets off Enron? Who would do that? Who would invest?

Fastow   Maybe nobody has to invest. We could make the company ourselves. I could use these raptor models. To make a sort of shadow company. A virtual Enron.

Skilling   We can't do business with ourselves –

Fastow   Of course not. But. The rules state, if we're gonna do business with another entity, it has to be *independent from us*.

Skilling   Exactly.

Fastow   But. Here's the kicker. To qualify as independent it just means *three per cent* of its capital has to come from independent sources.

Skilling   Only three per cent?

Fastow   Yeah, so ninety-seven per cent of a whole shadow company could just be … Enron stock.

Skilling   So Enron can do business with a company that's ninety-seven per cent Enron?

Fastow   Sure.

Skilling   Still gotta find that three per cent.

Fastow *is excitedy scoping out the room they are standing in.*

Fastow   Maybe. Look, say this entity, let's call it … LJM. If this room is LJM – it's filled with Enron stock, now we own that, we don't have to pay for and it's worth a great deal. *But* we need three per cent of it to be real. The equivalent of this file cabinet.

Fastow *walks around clearing the area to make the three per cent clear.*

Fastow   What if this three per cent is a smaller entity, designed the same way, which itself is made up of Enron stock –

Skilling   Except for three per cent.

Fastow   Yes, wait.

Fastow *opens the cabinet/table/desk to take out the shoe box which formerly housed his new shoes.*

Fastow   Here. But what if this three per cent is an even smaller entity …

He opens the shoe box.

Skilling   Made up of Enron stock …

Fastow   Except for three per cent!

Fastow *produces a matchbox.*

Skilling   On and on.

Fastow   Until for all this to be real, for this huge shadow company to exist, all we actually need …

Fastow *opens the matchbox and takes out a tiny red, glowing box.*

He holds it up, the men are bathed in it like some totem from an Indiana Jones film.

Fastow   Is this …

Skilling   And how much is that?

Fastow   Chump change. Few million.

Skilling   If that's a few million …?

Fastow   Imagine what the whole structure is worth, what it could do for Enron.

Skilling   It's made entirely of Enron stock …

Fastow (*brandishing tiny dot*)   Aaah, not entirely, this is what keeps it independent.

Skilling   But we can use it to *support* Enron stock, making sure it doesn't fall …

Fastow   Yup –

Skilling   The same stock that it's made of …?

Fastow   Yes.

Beat.

Skilling   That's fucking brilliant.

Fastow   It is, isn't it?

Skilling   So this shadow company, what did you call it –?

Fastow   LJM. After my wife and kids, Lea, Jeffrey and –

Skilling   This LJM can buy bad assets off Enron. And if anyone looks into it –

Fastow   It's just box after box after box. Russian dolls, until you get to …

The tiny box glows red and throbs.

Fastow   And who's gonna notice something as small as this? How's something this *tiny* ever gonna cause any trouble?

Skilling   Andy, you fucker! This is a whole new thing!

Fastow   And this is just a few million, hell, *I* could put that in.

Skilling   No, I don't like that.

Fastow   Oh. Okay.

Skilling   Doesn't that feel a bit cheap? A special purpose entity financed by the CFO?

Fastow   The CFO?

Skilling   Why not? Come on, we'll get banks to put that in; Wall Street money.

Fastow (*slightly surprised*)   Yeah, but don't we gotta check with our accountants?

Skilling   Sure.

Hey! Get me Arthur Andersen!

Arthur Andersen *appears to one side. He has a ventriloquist's dummy,* **Little Arthur**.

Arthur Andersen   As your accountant, we think this idea is:

Little Arthur   Poor to very poor.

Arthur Andersen   This is due to:

Little Arthur   Conflict of interest.

Fastow (*to* **Skilling**)   Well, maybe we just need a more sympathetic accountant.

Beat.

Skilling (*to* **Arthur Andersen**)   We could always take our business elsewhere.

Arthur Andersen's *dummy's eyes flit wildly.*

Arthur Andersen   Arthur Andersen will

Little Arthur   Approve

Arthur Andersen   Approve the strategy.

Little Arthur   If the lawyers approve.

Fastow   That's what we pay a million dollars a month for?

Skilling   Yeah, that's *exactly* what we pay a million dollars a month for.

I need the lawyers!

The law firm of **Ramsay** *and* **Hewitt** *appears to their other side; one male, one female. They appear as 'justice' with one blindfolded with sword, the other carrying the scales of justice.*

Ramsay   This is not a legal issue.

Hewitt   This is an accounting issue.

Skilling   The accountants say it's a legal issue.

Ramsay   Well, it was ever thus.

Hewitt   It's against your own code of conduct –

Ramsay   It's *their* code of conduct

Hewitt   Oh yes. Quite right. Your board could waive it.

Ramsay   Ask your board.

Hewitt   It's really not our business.

Ramsay and Hewitt   We'll bill you later on today.

Skilling   I need the board.

And then, revealed on the level above **Skilling** *and* **Fastow***, the board appear. The board is made up of shadowy, dark, imposing figures with the heads of mice and, in the centre,* **Ken Lay***.*

Skilling   The accountants and lawyers are okay with it if you're okay with it, Ken.

Lay   Oh, well in that case … One moment.

The board briefly consult.

Lay   Who's gonna run this thing?

Fastow   I will. I mean. I want to.

Lay   And who are you?

Fastow (*to* **Skilling**)   You know you won't find anyone you can trust like you trust me.

Lay   Young Andy Fastow?

Skilling (*arm round his protégé*)   He's our new Chief Financial Officer.

Fastow *is delighted at this.*

Lay   Okay(!)

Arthur Andersen   Okay?

Hewitt and Ramsay   Okay?

Lay   Okay?

Skilling   Okay?

Little Arthur   Okay.

Hewitt and Ramsay   Okay.

Lay   Okay.

Fastow   Okay!

All   Okay!

Lay   Here's to LJM.

Lay *signs papers in front of him.*

The board, **Arthur Andersen** *and* **Hewitt** *and* **Ramsay** *disappear.* **Fastow** *and* **Skilling** *hug in the centre.*

Skilling   You've saved my fucking life.

Fastow   It's good, isn't it?

Skilling   All I have to do is keep the stock price up.

Fastow   Which makes LJM exist.

Skilling   Which makes Enron strong.

Fastow   Which keeps the stock price up.

Skilling   It's better than good. It's perfect.

Scene Nine – Party Like It's 1999

Flashes from cameras.

A media event becomes a party filled with employees, press and analysts. It's a financial love-in.

Skilling *is being photographed for yet another magazine cover as the dynamic CEO changing the world. The* **Photographer** *is beneath him to make him look impressive, god-like.*

A **Reporter** *interviews him.*

News Reporter – Gayle   World's Most Innovative Company, how does that feel?

Skilling   I'm just pleased we're giving shareholders value for money.

News Reporter – Gayle   I guess it's a work hard, play hard sort of environment?

Skilling   We're aggressive, we take risks and that's why we're successful. Way I see it, if your executives aren't waking up at four in the morning, their heart beating out of their chest, they're not doing their job.

The **News Reporter** *flirts a bit.*

News Reporter – Gayle   Sure. So, here we are at the end of a millennium! Can you let me know what the next big innovation's gonna be?

Skilling   Well, I was gonna wait to announce this later tonight, but I'll give you a sneak preview. Video On Demand. We've teamed up with Blockbuster and Enron's gonna be streaming movies directly into your home by this time next year.

News Reporter – Gayle   Oh my god!

The stock price goes up.

Skilling *is approached by* **Lay.**

Lay   (Jeff, you know the congresswoman?)

Skilling   (Hi, great to meet you.)

Congresswoman   Hi, how are you?

Lay   Anne's been very useful for us up on the hill.

Congresswoman   Such a creative atmosphere. I'm thrilled to meet you, you're the expert in energy trading, right?

Lay   That's like saying Alexander Graham Bell knew about telephones. You're meeting the guy who invented the *concept.*

Congresswoman   Well we're all just thrilled to be here. I don't know how you're doing it, but you keep on doing it.

Split scene.

Below:

Fastow's *lair is revealed. He is finishing constructing LJM.*

LJM is a huge construct that has been designed to literally and metaphorically 'support' the level above it, Enron.

Fastow*, dressed in an even more dandy-ish fashion, is in his element.*

He takes calls on his phone. He's hugely in demand.

Fastow   Hi you're talking to Andy Fastow, Chief Financial Officer to the stars. Hey Rex you fuck, you know how many other divisions are begging for help with their numbers right now?! You're gonna have to hold. – Lou baby, now don't tell me bout your numbers – hey, I know those targets were unhittable, *I* know that. But you gonna take those losses? I didn't think so! No I'm not going up to the party. I leave my office the whole world falls apart, you know what

I mean? Don't worry. I'll make the numbers work. Everything's developing nicely down here.

Above:

Lay   Where's our Chief Financial Officer?

Skilling   Still working I guess.

Lay   No harm. He's hardly the life and soul –

Skilling   He's not a performer, he's got his own qualities.

Lay   Claudia thinks we should keep an eye on him.

Skilling   Oh for – seriously, Ken? You're listening to *her*!? She's jealous! Look around, all these ideas are mine!

Lay   It wasn't my intention –

Skilling   Broadband, electricity, energy trading, Video On Demand –

Concerned **Employees** *approach* **Skilling**.

Geek 1   Can we talk about Video On Demand?

Lay   Of course we can, sir, of course we can.

Who doesn't want movies streamed direct into their homes?

Geek 2   I don't think it's physically possible for next year.

Skilling   Video On Demand?

Geek 1   I can't see how it's possible at all.

Lay   I don't like that talk. That's unsupportive.

Skilling   We've got our best people working on it.

Geek 2   Sir, that's us.

Geek 1   We're the ones working on it.

Skilling   Tell me what you need and you'll get it.

Geek 1   It's not that –

Geek 2   It's about what's physically possible. There's not bandwidth capacity for it.

Skilling   Bandwidth?

Geek 2   It's the sort of … lines that internet information travels / along –

Skilling   / I know what the fuck bandwidth is. Buy as much as we need.

Geek 1   It doesn't work that way. There's a finite amount available.

Skilling   There's a finite amount?

Geek 1   Yeah.

Skilling   And people want it?

Both Geeks   Yeah(!)

Skilling *slaps the employees on the back. He turns back to the press interview.*

Skilling   Listen up, people, here's the next big thing: trading bandwidth.

Reporter   *Trading bandwidth?*

Skilling (*turns to everyone*)   Yeah, it's a hell of an Enron idea. If you're not using your bandwidth capacity, we can sell it on. It's tradeable. But people don't think in those terms because it's a virtual commodity. Well, Enron *gets* virtual. We're changing business, we're changing people's lives, we're changing the world.

Lay *applauds. The* **Employees** *are congratulated and sheepishly proud. The stock goes up hugely. Reaction is ecstatic, like a religious cult.* **Skilling** *is messiah-like.*

A huge party: absurd, luxurious, delusional; the peak of bull market excess. **Skilling** *shakes hands with everyone, treated like a movie star.*

Just then, **Roe** *makes a grand entrance to the party. Never one to be outshone, she is on a Harley motorbike, dressed entirely in leather.*

Skilling   You've got to be kidding me.

She shows off the back on which is stitched 'ENRON'. Whoops of celebration. She removes the helmet, revealing herself and shakes down her hair. Everyone loves it and all attention is lavished on her.

Skilling   This is what I'm talking about. Everything's the Claudia Roe show.

Lay   It's a very entertaining show!

Fireworks are starting to go off in the distance. The party reaches a peak of excitement as everyone goes upstairs to view them and celebratory opulence.

As everyone gets ushered out onto the balcony.

Below:

Fastow *hears/senses another presence in the lair of LJM.*

Fastow   Is someone down here? Hello?

Above:

Roe *marshals guests into place for the countdown she will be leading.*

Below, during:

Fastow *goes to seek out the source of the sound. Uncanny silence. He can sense someone … but where?*

Another movement from the opposite side … **Fastow** *swings around – what the …?*

And then, offstage, at the end of one of the streams of Raptor papers, he sees something hiding in the shadows.

Above:

Roe *begins a countdown to welcome in the new millennium. Others join in.*

Roe   Here we go!

Ten!

Nine!

Eight!

Seven!

Six!

Five!

Below, during:

Fastow *tensely, curiously approaches the shape. But, not wanting to get too close, he begins by reeling in the concertina-d string of papers it seems to be holding. Out of the shadows, a* **Raptor** *appears. It creeps forward, cocks its head and considers* **Fastow**. **Fastow** *stares back.*

Four!

Three!

Two!

One!

Above:

Roe *turns on the party's big event – the lighting up of a huge neon display welcoming in the new year: 2000.*

Below:

Fastow *turns slowly around to see the other two* **Raptors** *have taken corporeal form also and have crept into LJM.*

Fastow   Clever girls.

Blackout.

End of Act One

Interval

Fastow   No, but that's the thing, Jeff. I can! They're all so desperate to be seen alongside Enron. And who's Enron's CFO? Check it out.

Lehman Brothers   We were in talks about doing some *underwriting* work for Enron.

Fastow   For Enron?

Lehman Brothers   Yeah, we were hoping you'd consider giving us the contract –

Fastow   Way I see it, if I give you a contract worth tens of millions of dollars, least you can do is invest in a side project I got going on. Course Enron could take its business elsewhere –

Lehman Brothers   No, no, no, Andy, we heard. What you looking for?

Fastow   Let's start small, how 'bout ten million?

Lehman Brothers   Ten million! Everyone up at Enron okay with this, Jeff?

Skilling   What you asking me for?

Lehman Brothers   I mean, we assumed it was fine.

Skilling   You got a problem with LJM?

Lehman Brothers   Not at all.

Skilling   You got a problem with Andy?

Lehman Brothers   Well, he's got a certain –

Skilling   You do, you got a problem with me.

Lehman Brothers   No sir. Absolutely not. LJM's a real groundbreaking strategy.

The **Lehman Brothers** *give* **Fastow** *the money.*

Lehman Brothers   Nice doing business.

Fastow   Good job, fellas.

Act Two

Opening – Enron commercial with ethereal voices singing 'Why?'

Scene One – LJM

Fastow's *lair where LJM has been fully and complexly constructed.*

Among the shadows, there are strange movements going on. The **Raptors** *scuttle about. Not entirely human sounds. In the centre,* **Fastow**.

The tiny red box is safely put away, buried. We can see it throb. The **Raptors** *creep eerily around in the shadows.*

Skilling *enters. The* **Raptors** *hide.*

Skilling   Andy? Is everything right down here?

Fastow   Jeff! Everything's peachy.

Skilling   This place has got big.

Fastow   You won't believe the investment I got us. You wanted LJM to look official. Well? I've got fifteen million from JP Morgan, ten million Credit Suisse, five million from Merrill, everyone wants in with LJM –

Skilling   … Everyone wants to invest in our shadow? … Why?!

Two more figures emerge from the shadows: it is the **Lehman Brothers**.

Lehman Brothers   Hey, Mr Fastow!

Fastow   Oh, wait a second – it's the fucking Lehman Brothers. What do you guys want?

Lehman Brothers   We we were wondering …

Fastow   I'm busy here, what the fuck d'you want?

Skilling   That's one of the biggest investment banks in the world. You can't talk to them that way!

Skilling   Hey, Lehman Brothers!

The conjoined figures struggle to turn round in unison, both pulling in opposite directions. Eventually, they manage it.

Lehman Brothers   Yeeees?

Skilling   What's your analyst rating our stock at?

Lehman Brothers   Uh, Buy –

Skilling   Not Strong Buy?

Lehman Brothers   Not right … now.

Fastow   Let me.

Skilling *nods graciously.*

Fastow   If you rated us Strong Buy, more people would invest in Enron, right?

Lehman Brothers   I guess …

Fastow   And if more people invest in Enron, we can finance more projects, which makes Enron stronger and therefore …

Lehman Brothers   *Making* it / a strong buy …

Fastow   / A strong buy! See how it makes sense now?

Now, get the fuck out before I change my mind.

The **Lehman Brothers** *slink out.*

Skilling   I can't believe it. Everything upstairs is bullshit compared to this.

Fastow   I know! I think we've found the future of business … by accident.

Skilling   But where does all the debt go?

Sounds from the shadows.

Skilling   What's that?

Fastow   Nothing.

Skilling   What is it?

Fastow   Don't worry about it.

Skilling   What the fuck is this?

Skilling *goes to explore. One of the* **Raptors** *approaches* **Skilling** *to check him out. It smells him cautiously.*

Fastow   The raptors. You like 'em? They like you.

Skilling   That's where the debt goes …?

Skilling   These sort of entities, we could never have them publicly at Enron, but LJM doesn't need to show its books. We can … experiment here.

He feeds one of them a dollar bill.

Skilling   They're consuming our debt.

Fastow   Yes! Debt's just money. All money is debt.

Skilling   In … what … sense?

Fastow   If the bank gives you money, you owe *them*. You put money in the bank, they owe *you*.

All money is debt. It's just how you present it.

The **Raptors** *gain confidence at this and play with* **Skilling** *a little.*

Skilling   Go on.

Fastow   Okay. Well this one here, is dealing with Broadband. This one's taking care of Video On Demand while we set it up. And that one … that one's consuming all the fucking debt coming out of that rusting hulk of a power plant in Dabhol.

Skilling   That plant has no power coming out of it. It's surrounded by *protesters*. When Claudia makes a deal it doesn't just lose money, *people march against it.*

Fastow   You gotta put a stop to all that.

Skilling   She thinks her balls are cut off, what about my balls?!

Fastow   A man's got a right to his balls.

Skilling   *This* is the future. Not Claudia and her gift from grampa.

Beat.

Skilling   You think her numbers are right?

Fastow   Her division's numbers?

Skilling   Yeah. You think she's doing anything … untoward?

Fastow   I'd be surprised if there was *nothing* untoward. I mean, everybody … you know.

Beat.

Fastow   You want me to take a look?

Skilling   If you have cause for concern.

Fastow   Well sure, I mean. I can tell clever numbers. I'm the king of 'em(!)

Skilling *strokes a* **Raptor**.

Scene Two – The Purge

Roe *catches sight of a* **Raptor** *intimidating her.*

Roe (*to us*)   Something is happening to business. At the beginning of this century. Things have started to get divorced from the underlying realities. The best metaphor is this. Say we hold a competition here to determine who is the most beautiful woman in this room. Everyone gets a vote, the woman would be the one with the most votes and you'd win if you bet on her. Now the smart player wouldn't look at all the women in the room and choose the one he finds most beautiful. No, the smart player would try and imagine what a*verage opinion* would state is the most beautiful woman, and vote for her. But there's a level above that, where the really smart person would assume that most other people are doing the same thing and so they would try and choose the woman that *most other people* would think was *most other people's* idea of the most beautiful woman and vote for her. And there's even a level above that, and above that. And those are the values that determine prices, commodities and everybody's future. And who actually is the most beautiful woman in the room ... is irrelevant.

One of the **Raptors** *runs towards* **Roe** *and chases her out of the building.*

After a moment, **Lay** *enters* **Skilling**'s *office, looking pained.*

Skilling   Did you do it?

Lay   Still feel raw about that.

Skilling   I felt she had to hear it from you.

Lay   Can't recall what our thinking was there now.

Skilling   She wouldn't have taken it seriously from me.

Lay   I never did like letting people go.

You want to have a cigar?

Skilling   I'm good, thanks.

Lay *gives him one anyway.*

Lay   I was very disappointed in the things Claudia said in there. Didn't show a lot of class.

Skilling   Regarding what?

Lay   I don't believe she had to go so far in trying to save her own skin.

Skilling   I didn't want to have to bring those figures to your attention – I know they didn't look like much –

Lay   Any deceit is deceit. If something's brought before me I have to act on it. Doesn't *have* to be brought to me of course.

Skilling   Sure.

Lay   Now you made that decision and you brought it before me and a chain of events was put in place. Difficult to break that chain. You wanna pray with me, Jeffrey?

Pause.

Skilling   Sure.

Lay *bows his head in prayer, his hands together. He closes his eyes.* **Skilling** *copies him.*

After a few moments, **Lay** *has not spoken.* **Skilling** *opens his eyes. He watches* **Lay**, *not sure what to do.*

He watches **Lay**, *fascinated.*

After a little while, **Lay** *stops his silent prayers and raises his head.* **Skilling** *immediately tries to bow his to make it look like he hadn't stopped.*

Lay   Amen.

Skilling   It's a privilege.

Lay   Don't you worry, son.

You know how you tell the scout on a pioneer wagon?

Beat.

Lay   He's the one with all the arrows sticking out of him.

Beat. **Lay** *touches* **Skilling** *on the shoulder. It's a paternal, almost saintly action but takes* **Skilling** *by surprise.*

Lay   Listen, I know it's not been easy, having an old man on your back. You want to ride out, get the bit in your teeth and I'm all for that. I'm gonna take a step back. Place you can use me is on the board, on the Washington golf courses, charity luncheons. That's what I'm good at. You just carry on making us millions.

Skilling   We really gotta get deregulation moving. That's how we're gonna make our money.

Lay   I'm gonna have more talk with Junior. I got hope for him yet.

Skilling   We're financing that whole campaign. If he doesn't come through –

Lay   These things take time. Government! Can't even smoke these indoors anymore.

Skilling   You can do what you want, Ken.

Lay   Can't even smoke indoors.

Lay *drifts off. Pause.* **Skilling** *picks up the cigar he left him.*

Scene Three – Rooftop

Roe *is having a last cigarette outside on the rooftop / terrace of the Enron building.*

Skilling *comes out.*

Roe *has been crying. She hastily attempts to cover any sign of her tears.*

Skilling   You're not gonna jump are you, Claud? /

Roe   / Fuck you.

Skilling   I'll leave you alone.

Roe   Don't move. Don't you dare go anywhere.

Skilling   You can go and get any number of jobs –

Roe   I WANT TO WORK HERE!

This is where I work!

Skilling   Not anymore.

Roe   That man had faith in me for fifteen years. I've given my life to this company. You had him come in and talk to me like I'm some thieving kid in his store.

Skilling   I asked Ken because I thought it would be worse for me to fire you –

Roe   I was not fired! I resigned. You show me one part of my numbers done differently from anyone else here – you lied to get me out.

Skilling   I didn't have to lie. You're an amateur.

Roe   We'll see about that.

Skilling   Did you tell Ken something I should know about …?

Roe   There's rumours. Is it true Broadband and Electricity aren't bringing in any money? That Video On Demand doesn't even have the technology developed?

Skilling   Why do people talk that way? We'll make those profits. It's like playing poker with these guys who get mad when you win on the last card, 'Why did you stay in? You're not playing properly!' It's *poker*, you idiot. Doesn't matter how you win – as long as you win! When electricity gets deregulated, the cash flow –

Roe   Oh, grow the fuck up. Electricity won't be deregulated! Ken's not gonna get that kid in the White House!

Skilling   We will.

Roe   I could have made India work! All your deals getting done all the time, bad deals. Sign it, book it, throw it over the fence. Doesn't matter if it's a bad deal, just get the deal done.

Skilling   You don't know anything.

Roe   I know you.

You know when you went to that college in Pennsylvania.

Skilling   I went to Harvard.

Roe (*shakes head*)   When your father showed you round his old college in Bethlehem, Pennsylvania. You told me about it our first night. You looked out that window saw all those abandoned steel mills, for miles. All that dead industry. That grey sky.

Skilling   I left all that behind.

Roe   No. That's what you're creating now.

Skilling   Get out of my building.

Roe   You know what I'm gonna do? I'm gonna go home, to my beautiful children. And I'm gonna sell every single one of my shares.

She stubs her cigarette out. She leaves him.

His **Daughter** *blows bubbles somewhere on stage.*

Daughter   One, two, three, four, five –

Skilling   I have to check the stock price.

Daughter   Why?

Skilling   Because that's how Daddy knows how much he's worth.

Daughter   Why?

Skilling   Well, the market knows how many people believe in Daddy. And that's important.

Daughter   Why?

Skilling   It's important because I want people to like me. I don't want them to go round saying bad things.

Daughter   Why?

Skilling   Because in business these things matter.

Daughter   Why?

Skilling   Because it's important to look strong. That's the first thing.

Daughter   Why?

Skilling   That's how we make money.

Daughter   Why?

Skilling   Because I want to provide for you.

Daughter   Why?

Beat.

Skilling   Because I love you. Now let Daddy go to work.

Skilling *turns to his daughter but she has disappeared, leaving only bubbles in her wake.*

Scene Four – The American Spirit

Skilling *gives a speech to* **Employees**.

Skilling   Our stock is so strong. So strong that I think all employees should have the opportunity to benefit. I want to extend the stock option to everybody. From the mail room all the way up.

Employee   Why be paid in stock and not cash?

Skilling   Because if you're invested in the company you work for you are literally investing in yourself – it is an act of belief in yourself. Which you should all have. Because, I believe in you. So, grab that opportunity. Now, tonight's a big night for us. I hope you've all voted. I don't know if you know, but we got a local boy in the race(!)

Laughter. They are now looking up concentrating on an image of America on screens.

Election coverage:

The screen goes red.

INDIANA CALLED FOR BUSH

+ 12

They cheer.

Screen turns blue

VERMONT CALLED FOR GORE

+3

They boo.

FLORIDA

They inhale.

TOO CLOSE TO CALL.

Scene Five – Andy's Lair of LJM

Skilling *enters.* **Fastow** *is with the* **Raptors** *watching the election results roll in.*

Skilling   You got it on down here?

Fastow   Sure. We're having a party.

Fastow *has a bottle of champagne he's swigging from. He's surrounded by his* **Raptors**. *They all stare at the screen.*

An electoral map of the United States on screen.

ALABAMA: TOO CLOSE TO CALL (GAYLE)

Skilling   *Alabama* too close to call?! You gotta be fucking kidding me.

Fastow   Hey, it's early.

Skilling   I'm going crazy with this.

Fastow   Hey, they're calling my baby –!

It's blue.

NEW JERSEY: CALLED FOR GORE (GAYLE)

+ 15

Fastow   Goddamn you, New Jersey. I love you but you break my fucking heart.

Beat.

Skilling   Now we got the big boys –

Fastow   Lone star!

It's red.

TEXAS: CALLED FOR BUSH (GAYLE)

+ 32

Fastow   Come on!

Skilling   Yeah but here goes the other side.

It's blue.

CALIFORNIA: CALLED FOR GORE (GAYLE)

+ 54

Fastow   (Surprise!)

Skilling   It's all about Florida.

Beat.

FLORIDA: CALLED FOR GORE (GAYLE)

+ 25

Fastow   No.

Beat.

Skilling   (Fuck fuck fuck.)

Fastow   What about Colorado, we might get Colorado.

Skilling   What the fuck we want with Colorado, eight fucking votes. This is chicken shit. Game's over.

Fastow   Hey, we've had eight years of this shit, we'll have eight more –

Skilling   No, Andy, you don't know. Clinton's been real good to us. This guy … this guy scares me.

Fastow   Scares you!? Come on, man –

Skilling   That's it. We're done.

Fastow   Have a little faith.

Skilling   Faith?! Andy, you gotta understand. I don't have any cash. I can't operate. I have no money.

Fastow (*shock*)   You, personally?

I got money – I can –

Skilling   Not me *personally*, Andy, you prick. What, you think I'm some drinking, gambling it away prick can't find cash on my salary? What is it you think?!

Fastow   No, no, I …

We'll get through this.

Skilling   Without someone friendly to us right now, we're dead.

Skilling *seems to be in pain; his stomach.*

Skilling   I haven't been sleeping. People need to get paid.

Fastow   Pay them in stock, with our stock price –

Skilling   Everyone *is* paid in stock. Already, *that's why it can't go down* –

Fastow   No, it can't. This whole set up is / founded on the stock price –

Skilling   / I know!

Fastow   Are you saying it's going down?

Skilling   I'm saying it *can't* go / down.

Fastow   / That's what I'm saying.

Skilling   Well, stop telling me what I already / know!

Fastow   / I'm trying to make it work here!

Skilling   Well that's your fucking job, ain't it?

Beat.

Skilling   (Sorry.)

Fastow   You need capital. You need the cash. One, two, three?

Skilling   More like four –

Fastow   Four million I can find …

Skilling *stares at him.*

Skilling   Million?! No.

Beat.

Fastow   You need four *billion* dollars? Cash?

Beat.

Skilling   We're the world's most innovative company. How can we not find four / billion dollars?!

Fastow   / That's not what I do. This is all … this is *structured finance*. This is how it *looks* … I can't make real money just *appear.*

Skilling (*losing control*)   Then what good are you …? What fucking good is any of this to me?! Then we're going down, Andy / and it's your –

Fastow   / Wait, –

Screens go red.

(GAYLE)

RECOUNT: FLORIDA CALLED FOR BUSH

Skilling   What does that mean?

Fastow   If you need actual capital …

Skilling   But they called it for Gore.

Fastow   If you need cash coming in the door, actual cash then you need to sell something real …

Skilling   I've sold everything!

So what, have we won?!

Fastow   Fox says yes!

Skilling   CNN says no.

Screens go blue.

FLORIDA RETRACTED FROM BUSH (GAYLE)

Fastow   No!

Skilling   What the fuck are they doing?

Fastow   Well they gotta decide.

Skilling   What's going on out there?!

Fastow   Someone has to call this.

Skilling   What dumbass is running this thing?

Fastow   They can't do this. If there's one thing this country won't stand for it's ambiguity.

Flicking through channels.

Fastow   Who's won? Who's / won?!

Skilling   / Who's won!?

Just then, **Lay** *enters, hanging up on a phone call. He is deliberately oblivious to the strange, exaggerated world of LJM. The* **Raptors** *scuttle away.*

Lay   Gentlemen. Guess who's just got off a call with the next President of the United States?

Skilling   Say we got a Texan in the White House.

Skilling *is clutching his stomach.*

Lay   Like father like son.

Skilling *falls to his knees with the relief.*

Lay   *And* we got ourselves a deregulated state to play with.

Fastow   *There's* your cash!

Skilling   A small state, or …?

News Report   The state of California has announced it's going to be the first state to implement a deregulated electricity market.

Video footage of George W. Bush being sworn in as President of the United States.

Scene Six – Texas vs California

The floor is flooded with **Traders**.

During the following, **Traders** *are manipulating California's electricity market by moving energy around. It should be tremendous fun, extremely fast, physical and overlap is encouraged.*

Skilling (*addressed to the* **Traders**)   Gentlemen. We've finally got our chance to move out all across the country. This is about freedom. This is about competition. A deregulated system means one thing and one thing only controls electricity. *The market*. I'm setting you free in California, fellas, bring it on home.

Trader 8   Okay traders! We're going to get a little … 'creative'. We're free to move power around. Take it out of the state. Move it out so the price goes *up*! Then, who they gonna run to?

Trader 3   California! Yes, people, an electricity market of such complexity, designed by people of such simplicity. Loopholes so big you could fuck a fat chick through 'em and neither of you touch the sides. Let's find arbitrage opportunities. Let's. Fucking. Play.

All right man, this is Clem up at Enron. We're buying as much electricity as we can and taking it out of the state.

Trader 4   Ricochet! Fat Boy! Burn Out! Death Star!

Trader 2   Hollywood wants their power back? Fucking *pay*!

Trader 6   There's a party in the desert, man, and we need it for the lights!

Trader 7   Wheeling electricity out of the state, push the prices up, get 'em high –

Trader 4   Sell it back when they're desperate!

Trader 5   The most beautiful thing about electricity –?

All Traders   It cannot be stored!

Trader 4   Holy shit, price is up through a hundred!

They all look.

Trader 1   I've never seen prices like these –

Trader 5   Welcome to the beautiful state of Californ-I-A!

Trader 6   We're making billions of dollars!

All Traders   For Enron!

Laughter.

News Report   (California's power supply came up short today, and the lights went out. Rolling blackouts have hit the sixth largest economy in the world. For the first time in sixty-five years, the electric power market is in chaos. Electricity rates are climbing and California has gone into meltdown.)

Trader 5   There's a fire on the core line!

Trader 2   More fires we have, more prices go up!

All Traders   Burn baby burn!

News Reporters (Gayle, Elise)   (Another day another death in the story of California's blackouts. The driver of a station wagon was killed early Friday when she collided with a transit bus at an Oakland intersection where the traffic lights were down. This after surgeons were left without operating lights in San Pablo forcing patients to be air-lifted out of state –)

Laughter.

Skilling   We are doing the right thing in California. I mean, people are saying we shouldn't trade electricity – do you really believe that? Let's, let's stop trading wheat. Let's stop trading – you know, we need automobiles to maintain the logistics system, so does that mean we can't trade steel? We are the *good guys* in California. We are on the side of angels.

Physical sequence.

News Reporters   (Today the governor of California, Gray Davis, declared a *state of emergency* after being forced to cut power for hundreds of thousands of people throughout the state.)

Lay (*on phone*)   Kenneth Lay here for the governor of California. Governor! I understand you're considering running for president. You think it's gonna help you any to have the sixth largest economy in the world go dark on your watch? Voters remember that sort of thing. So how 'bout paying the prices we're asking?

Well I'm sorry to hear you say that, Governor.

Lay *hangs up the phone.*

Lay (*to* **Traders**)   Boys, step it up.

Trader 5   Come on!!

Physical sequence.

A crescendo of sound and activity is being reached. It builds and builds.

Trader 1   This is the largest single transfer of wealth I've ever seen!

Trader 7   We're like the Roman empire! We're going fucking down!

Trader 4   Let's rape this muthafucker!

Trader 5   Push it through the fucking roof.

Trader 1   Okay, okay!

Trader 8   / Do it, do it!

Everyone and everything is at fever pitch, yelling and encouraging.

A climax.

Skilling   You know the difference between the state of California and the *Titanic*? At least when the *Titanic* went down the lights were on.

Every light in the world seems to go out.

Utter darkness everywhere. For a shade longer than is comfortable.

And then …

Nothing but the light from a small doorway.

In front of the light of the doorway, a man comes into view. It is the figure of **Ken Lay**. *A suited man comes on stage and goes through the door, first shaking* **Lay**'s *hand.*

Lay   Hi, Mr Mayor, I'm sure we can get this blackout business under control.

Another suited man approaches the door. **Lay** *shakes hands with him.*

Lay   Thanks for coming out.

Another suited man right behind him, shakes **Lay**'s *hand and goes in.*

Lay   Don't worry, I got just the guy to fix this.

And then, another suited man approaches. He is huge and square and muscular in his suit. **Lay** *looks up at him, His face breaking into a grin. They shake hands. The man's broad back fills the doorway.*

Lay   Mr Schwarzenegger! I'm so glad you could make it. Now, let's go inside and talk about the future of California.

Arnold Schwarzenegger *steps in to the meeting, followed by* **Lay**.

The door closes.

Scene Seven – Skilling's Office

Skilling   I hate those guys. I hate those legislators and politicians – not because they restrict business and fuck up the markets, even though they do and it does. I hate government because I know those guys. I went to school with them. And let me tell you, the weakest, most ignorant, most drunken fucking incompetents went to work for the US government. Because they weren't smart enough for the private sector. And that's the truth. I got head hunted. And those bottom of the fucking barrel, frat party know-nothing fucks who never got the call *design* the regulations for an energy market they know nothing about. It's my *job* to find ways round that. Why should we respect ineptitude? Why should we look at the lazy fucking regulations they've put in place by committee and go, 'yeah, you suck at your jobs, fine, we'll ignore that and just suck at ours too.' Who do you think is gonna win in the end?! The greedy or the inept?! We're not perfect, but wait til you see the other guys.

Skilling *is in a meeting with the* **Lawyer**.

Lawyer   Understood.

Skilling   So why the fuck are people picketing my house!?

Lawyer   There were deaths in California. If I'm gonna represent you I need to know your level of involvement.

Skilling   I want you to represent me, not the company. I didn't kill anyone.

Lawyer   There may be civil suits against *you.*

Skilling   This is crazy.

Lawyer   I can find other companies that were out there doing this. But you're getting the bad press cos your guys gave it a name.

Skilling   What do you mean?

Lawyer (*consults his papers*)   Ricochet. Fat Boy. Burn Out. Death Star. All on record as your traders' names for their strategies in California.

Skilling   Death Star?!

Lawyer   What I'm saying. 'Death Star' – makes it sound like kids on a video game.

Skilling   That's a perception problem.

Lawyer   Jeff, sending a state into *chaos* is, you know, that's more than just a perception problem.

Skilling   Will this affect the stock price?

Lawyer   I'm a lawyer, not a stock analyst.

Skilling   Cos that cannot happen.

Lawyer   Maybe you should have thought of that before.

Skilling   But we didn't do anything illegal in California.

Lawyer   That's a matter of opinion.

Skilling   I got a group of the smartest people in the world here who can tell you why what they did was *not* illegal.

Lawyer   If it wasn't illegal, it was stupid.

Skilling   I don't think you understand how markets work.

Lawyer   I'm not interested in the economics.

Skilling   So what are you interested in?

Lawyer   Protecting you.

They're going to imply that your traders caused huge blackouts in California for months, maybe years. That you gamed the state –

Skilling   The state's regulations were a mess.

Lawyer   And you took advantage of that?

Beat.

Skilling   Took advantage of that. Are you kidding me(?) Took advantage of … (!) That's what we *do*. In business, you buy something at one price, you sell it at a higher one and what's in between, that's your advantage. Which you *take*. That's how the world *works*. If you want an objective morality present in every contract you're living in a dream. You know how difficult it is to get five people in a room to agree *anything*? The only way I can be sure I can *trust* a contract is cos every party's in it for themselves. So when you ask, 'did we take *advantage* of that'(!) … You know what I hear? I hear, do you make a living, do you breathe in and out, are you a man? So yes, we took advantage of that. And I know that the only difference between me and the people judging me is they weren't smart enough to do what we did. Now are you going judge me or are you going to help me?

Lawyer   There'll be a couple of guys in trading will take a fall, they'll get a little wire fraud. There'll only be a bigger problem if there's anything else, any underlying …

Skilling   Okay. Okay.

A large Enron **Security Officer** *appears in* **Skilling**'s *doorway.*

Skilling *shakes the* **Lawyer**'s *hand.*

Security Officer   You wanted me to take a look at something?

Skilling   Yes, please. Yeah.

Lawyer   I'll take care of it.

Skilling   Thanks.

The **Lawyer** *leaves.*

Security Officer   Sir.

Skilling   Hey.

Sorry, this is a little – can you, can you sweep this office for … equipment or recording …

Security Officer   You think you're being bugged, sir?

Skilling   Maybe, something –

Security Officer   That might be a matter for the FBI –

Skilling   No, no, just take a look –

Security Officer   You think it's the government, sir?

Skilling   No –

Security Officer   A rival company –

Skilling   I don't know. I just got a feeling.

The **Security Officer** *checks around the office surfaces.*

Skilling   How's things in maintenance?

Security Officer   I'm in security, sir.

Skilling   Sure.

Security Officer   It's good.

Skilling   You all got your 401Ks? You're all okay?

Security Officer   Absolutely, sir. I got a daughter and I'd like her to go to college, do something real … Well, things become a lot easier with the stock options you've given us, that becomes a possibility.

Skilling   Yeah. Good.

Listen, can you hear, like a hiss like, you can tell something's on? … . Wait, maybe under …

Skilling *gets down on the floor. He eventually puts his ear near the floor.*

Skilling   Here.

The **Security Officer** *gets down on the floor too. He copies* **Skilling** *who puts his ear to floor. They listen, lying on the floor together.*

Skilling   There's a sort of, ticking sound.

They listen …

Security Officer   Might that be your watch, sir?

Skilling'*s head is leaning on his wrist with his watch on. He gets up, embarrassed.*

Skilling   It was earlier.

Security Officer   Could be something just needs rewiring, sometimes a static charge / – (can build up)

Skilling   / Yeah.

Security Officer   Well, you let me know if you hear anything.

Skilling   Sure.

It's hot out, don't you think?

Security Officer   Real dry. The trees are bribing the dogs.

They laugh.

Skilling   Hey. You'll be straight. I've been thinking about our next venture. I've been thinking about taking Enron into weather.

Security Officer   Weather?

Skilling   Yeah, for investors or companies whose worth can be damaged by bad weather. We could carve out a market in protecting against that. Have people buy up shares in weather.

Security Officer   Like insurance?

Skilling   Sort of, yeah. We break up the risk, sell it off in parts like credit derivatives.

Security Officer   You're losing me, sir.

Skilling (*keen, looking for paper and pen*)   Sit down. I can explain it to you in minutes.

Security Officer   Sounds a little out of my –

Skilling   It makes total sense –

Security Officer   I just want to do my job.

Skilling   You don't want to hear what's next for the company?

Security Officer   You're telling me to –

Skilling   Sit down! You want to be a doorman the rest of your life? Sit down and listen!

Beat.

Security Officer   I'm a security officer, sir.

Skilling   Sure, I know.

Security Officer   I just got a shift I gotta do is all.

Skilling   I just wanted you to understand …

Beat.

Security Officer   Nothing to it. We trust you all up here, sir …

Skilling   Very Enron though. Dealing in weather?

Security Officer   Sure. It's your company, sir. You run it how you want it run.

Skilling *nods.*

Security Officer *leaves.*

Skilling's *intercom beeps.*

Skilling   Yes?

Secretary (*V.O.*)   Mr Skilling, there's a reporter on the line from *Fortune* magazine –

The stock price sinks. **Skilling**'s *face falls.*

Skilling (*down phone*)   Jeff Skilling.

I can't answer those questions right now. I am not an accountant. Look, I don't think you understand the complexity of the way we operate here. If you print an article now without our side, I personally think that's unethical. Sure, I'll send someone out, at Enron's expense. He'll fly out and help you understand the questions you're asking. Okay.

He hangs up.

Skilling   Goddamn.

Scene Eight – Andy's Lair

Skilling *enters* **Fastow**'s *shady lair, all anxiety.*

The **Raptors** *stay out. Two have grown very bold now – fast and aggressive. One of them is weak and sickly, the other two flank it to protect it.*

Skilling *approaches to pet them and one of the strong raptors is aggressive. He backs off, it follows him and pins him.*

Skilling *is deeply unnerved by them.*

Skilling   Andy?!

No reply.

Skilling   Andy!

Fastow *enters.*

Fastow   Hey.

Skilling *swings around. There is something eerie about* **Fastow***.*

Fastow *tazers a* **Raptor** *to protect* **Skilling***. It falls down, ultimately unharmed. The others back off.*

Skilling   What the fuck was that …?

Fastow   Something's spooked 'em.

Skilling   What's wrong with that one?

Fastow   It's sick. I don't know. Maybe I gave it too much.

Skilling   Too much what?

Fastow   Hmm? Oh, of the debt, Jeff.

Skilling   Will it spread?

Fastow   No. I don't know.

Fastow *tries to look at and comfort the injured* **Raptor***.*

Skilling   Well. That's a good reason. That's a good excuse, we're getting rid of them.

They seem to hear him and snap around, maybe moving towards **Fastow** *for support.*

Fastow   Jeff?!

Skilling   You heard me.

Fastow   We can't. They're consuming a billion dollars' worth of debt.

Skilling   Get rid of them.

Beat.

I need you to fly out to New York.

Fastow   What's in New York?

Skilling   A reporter. *Fortune* magazine. They're running an article on us.

Fastow   A reporter wants to talk to me!

Skilling   It's not a positive article.

Fastow   What do you mean it's not a positive article?!

Skilling   They have *questions.*

Fastow   Fuck them! We don't have to –

Skilling   You got to go out there and explain how it works. How money flows through the business. That we're not a black box.

Fastow   But we *are* a black box, Jeff.

Skilling   We are not! We're a logistics company! With a ton of great ideas –

Fastow   I don't want to leave LJM.

Skilling   You're going and you're / (gonna) –

Fastow   / Please don't make me go.

Skilling   You're Chief Financial Officer –

Fastow   Jeff, I'm at my best here.

Skilling (*violent*)   Be a fucking man! You're going to have to choose between LJM and Enron.

Fastow   I created LJM.

Skilling   I created *you*!

Andy, I love you. And I would do anything for you. But you're gonna have to choose.

Beat.

Fastow   What am I gonna say?!

Skilling   Look, if we disclose everything, there'll be panic, right?

Fastow   Right.

Skilling   So for everyone's good, they don't want trouble, we don't want trouble –

Fastow   What if they *do* want trouble, Jeff? I mean, they're a *magazine*. What if they take a look, what if they take a *really close look* and they come to the conclusion that everything's just *hedged* against our *own stock* –

Skilling   Don't you dare say that in my (presence) –

Fastow   What if they look and they see that underneath there's *nothing actually there* / –

Skilling   / Nothing?! Twenty thousand employees taking home paychecks nothing? World's most innovative company? – We *run* Texas, is that nothing? Then the whole fucking thing's nothing. Then the world's nothing.

As **Skilling** *is at his most manic and the* **Raptors** *are circling,* **Ken Lay** *enters.*

Lay   Hey, Jeff! Here you are. Listen, I need your opinion. I don't know which of these for the cabin of the new jet.

He holds the choices up. Both men stare at him.

Skilling (*slowly*)   Andy has to fly out to New York.

Fastow   There's a loss of confidence. I think. Going on.

Lay   So I'm hearing. I'll talk to Dick.

Skilling   That won't do it. Ken, this has all been across your desk, you know what's / going on.

Lay   / Listen, if you boys are talking business –

Fastow   I mean, I was only doing what I was asked to do.

Skilling   And if the stock falls –

Lay   The stock is not going to fall. That is not going to happen. You're running this show, Jeff.

Skilling   We need to have a conversation / –

Lay (*threatening*)   I don't want to have a conversation! Once you bury a dead dog, you don't dig it up to smell it!

Now, which goddamn pattern?

Lay *doesn't look at the* **Raptors** *or anything except the material swatches and sometimes* **Skilling**.

Skilling, *desperately buying into the charade, points at one.* **Lay** *nods, satisfied and lowers the swatches.*

Lay   Okay. Okay, listen up. This is a confidence thing. You're gonna have to make a call with the stock analysts to reassure the market. This is just a confidence thing.

Beat.

Lay   Now!

Skilling, *dead-eyed, gets ushered off.*

Fastow   Okay, okay! I'll go! I'll just take all the paperwork. Throw information at them. Bury them / in it!

Lay *turns back, eyes the minion.*

Lay   You don't belong to me, boy.

Lay *leaves.*

Left alone with his creations, **Fastow** *rallies himself to do his master's bidding. He eyes the* **Raptors**.

Fastow   I'm sorry girls. I gotta take you off the books.

Fastow *approaches the wary* **Raptors**.

Fastow   I don't care what they say about the company. As long as they don't make me look bad.

Fastow *destroys the* **Raptors** *and torches LJM.*

Scene Nine – The Asshole

Skilling *climbs stairs like a man on his way to the gallows, unkempt and addled.*

He eyes the stock price.

Lay Everyone just needs a bit of faith restored. Stand straight, Jeffrey. You couldn't shave?

Skilling I know. I'm fine. I'm Jeff Skilling. Okay.

Lay Here we go.

As they go up, analysts and journalists emerge from everywhere to listen to the conference call.

Skilling Just an outstanding quarter, another outstanding quarter. We're growing real quick in earnings and revenue and we have the strongest position in every market we're in … You know, so I have no idea why our stock's as low as it is, fifty-four dollars, that's crazy! People are saying we're opaque, we're a black box, we're not. That's like calling Michael Jordan a black box just cos you don't know what he's gonna score each quarter! We are very optimistic …

Silence. **Skilling** *exhales.*

Lay You'll take questions now.

Skilling I'll take questions now.

Analyst (Grubman) Hi, Richard Grubman here, hello.

Skilling Mr Grubman.

Analyst (Grubman) Hello. I don't really care about the earnings at this point. What I want to see is a balance sheet.

Skilling We will have that done shortly. But until we put all that together, we just cannot give you that.

Analyst (Grubman) I am trying to understand why that would be an unreasonable request.

Skilling   I'm not saying we can't tell you what the balances are. But we'll wait – at this point – to disclose those until all … the right accounting is put together.

Analyst (Grubman)   You're the only financial institution that cannot produce a balance sheet or a cash flow statement with their earnings.

Skilling   Well, you're … you – well, uh, thank you very much. We appreciate it.

Analyst (Grubman)   *Appreciate* it?

Skilling   Asshole.

There is utter silence as everyone realizes what he just said to an important stock analyst.

Everyone looks at each other. The silent shock of a tumbleweed moment.

As the call is cut, **Skilling** *looks over the edge of the upper level, looking for all the world like he's either about to be sick or throw himself off.*

Pause.

Business Anchor (Gayle)   Shockwaves were sent through the market today as Chief Executive of Enron, Jeffrey Skilling referred to a senior stock analyst with a common but offensive term.

The analysts all get on their phones and BlackBerries to their banks and brokerage firms

Analysts (*together, overlapping, merging into one*)   You're never gonna guess what the fuck just happened – I think the big JS is losing it here – You got share price on Enron? – Something's going on down there – Called a Wall Street analyst an 'a-hole' during a conference call – CEO's gone sorta postal – I'm gonna recommend we hold – I don't know for now – I'm hearin stuff here I don't like – Enron, the energy company – I want to ask for the books – Rumours they're a black box. You wanna sell? – I wanna sell – Are people selling? – Okay, we're outta there – Hold on

Enron – Sell – Hold – Sell – Somebody selling – Enron – Sell – Hold – Okay – Selling – What's the market doing? – Hold – Selling – Enron – Sell – Sell – Selling Enron, Enron – 'Asshole, asshole, asshole.'

The **Analysts** *have taken themselves off, hurrying back to their marketplace hubs, a sea change in the offing.*

But their effects are already painfully clear on the stockprice, which is freefalling.

A spotlight on **Skilling** *alone, unsupported. Just him and his representation of his self-worth, the stock price.*

Skilling *approaches it desperately, trying to regain former glories.*

Skilling   No! Come on. I'm happy, I'm … excited …

The stock price does not respond.

Skilling   Come on, this is crazy.

Nothing.

Skilling   IT'S ME! Everything will be fine, don't be idiotic!

The stock price drops slightly. **Skilling** *recoils with shock.*

Skilling   No, no, no, sorry –

It drops further. He's terrified.

Skilling   Jesus, no, stop. Oh god.

He goes to his phone. He calls a number. A moment.

Skilling   Hi, sweetheart. It's your dad. Are you okay? Yeah, I'm sorry, I know, it's four in the morning. Is your mom there?

Beat.

Skilling   Okay, well, this is important. I need you to tell her something. Are you awake? Okay. Tell her to sell her shares. Sell her shares. All of them. Okay. I love you.

He turns to the stock price.

Skilling   What do you want? You want me? Is that it? Is that what you want?!

He ends, his arms outstretched, crucifying himself before the market.

The blocks beneath where **Skilling** *was standing are removed by analysts and brokers as shares continue to be sold and the company weakens.*

A sour, tuneless version of the Enron barbershop quartet jingle plays.

Scene Ten – Private Meeting

Sheryl Sloman *and* **Ken Lay** *are in a meeting with* **Skilling**.

Sloman (*to* **Skilling**)   You're resigning?

Lay   We wanted to tell you first.

Sloman   When are you going public with this?

Lay   Later on today. We don't want the market getting the wrong idea. You've always been a great cheerleader for us.

Sloman   I'm a professional stock analyst. Let's not pretend, Jeff. This is highly unusual. There should be a *year* leading up to this, a structured handover. Jeff, *why* are you resigning?

Skilling (*teary*)   The company's in great shape it couldn't be less to do with that. I … A company like this, it consumes your life. I've neglected my daughter. This is personal.

Lay   It's not cos of the stock.

Skilling   I'm doing this for the company. It'll go up when I announce. The market's decided. It wants me out.

Sloman   But that's not true. People say all over, I'm not long Enron, but I'm long Jeff Skilling.

This seems to affect him deeply.

Skilling   You pour your life into something and, if it doesn't reflect back at you … I'm so tired.

I can't sleep.

Sloman   Are you worried about recent performance? Are there accounting issues /?

Lay   / There are no accounting / issues –

Sloman (*to* **Skilling**)   / Is that why you can't sleep?

Skilling   I haven't slept since I was fourteen.

Lay   I can honestly say the company's in the best shape it's ever been.

Jeff?

Skilling thinks he sees a **Raptor** *still at large in the bowels of Enron.*

Skilling   I should go.

Lay   Yeah, you go, get ready to announce.

Skilling *leaves.*

Sloman   Whoo. This is a blow for you.

Lay (*understating*)   I would have preferred he stay.

Sloman   That *Fortune* article raised a lot of questions. I've always been a supporter of Enron Corporation. But you know the CEO leaving like this? That doesn't spin.

You're gonna have to hold this thing together.

Lay   Don't you worry about anything here. I'm a safe pair of hands.

With a reassuring squeeze of her arm, **Lay** *stalks off, leaving* **Sloman** *thoughtful.*

News Reporters   In breaking news, Enron's CEO has resigned. Now the market's left asking the question the company is famous for: Why?

Act Three

Scene One – The Earthquake Hits

Sloman (*to us*)   There's a strange thing goes on inside a bubble. It's hard to describe. People who are in it can't see outside of it, don't believe there is an outside. You get glazed over. I believed in Enron. Everybody did. I told people again and again to keep buying that stock and I kept rating it and supporting it and championing it like it was my own child. And people say how could you. If you didn't understand how it worked. Well. You get on a plane, you don't understand exactly how it works, but you believe it'll fly. You know – and everyone else boarding that plane knows – it'll fly up into the air and take you to your destination, crazy as that may seem. And if you got out your seat, said I'm not flying, I don't understand how it works, you'd look crazy. Well it's like that. Except. Imagine if the *belief* that the plane could fly was all that was keeping it in the air. It'd be fine. If everybody believed. If nobody got scared. As long as people didn't ask stupid questions. About what it is keeps planes in the air.

September 11th 2001.

Eventually …

Ken Lay *comes out to give a speech.*

As the speech goes on, **Lay** *becomes surrounded by tiny piece of shredded paper being blown all over him, all over the stage. He keeps trying to carry on regardless. The shredding represents the huge destruction of documents going on at Enron and Arthur Andersen.*

Lay   Well, I'm delighted to be back in charge. In more normal circumstances, I'd have a few words to say about September the 11th. Just like America's under attack by terrorism, I think we're under attack, at Enron.

News Report (Gayle)   The terror attacks on New York and Washington have seen stock exchanges all over the world evacuated and all trading has ceased. Market confidence has dissolved today as Tokyo, London and then New York fell to record lows –

Lay   I'm sorry Jeff did resign. Despite the rumours, the company is doing well both financially and operationally. When our very way of life is being threatened, we remain proud of who we are and what we do. This is not the time for doubt, not the time for our confidence to be shaken –

News Report (Elise)   (With the world's markets still reeling from the recent tragic events, a formal investigation has been opened into energy trading giant Enron, deepening its share price crisis. The company has lost 60 per cent of its value since peaking last fall …)

Lay   Truth is the great rock. Whether it will continue to be submerged by a wave – a wave of terror by those attacking us – will be determined by Enron employees. We will testify to the truth. We will let the light shine in. We won't let this cloud of lies cover all our good works and deeds.

Collapse.

News Report (Gayle)   Today saw the largest corporate bankruptcy in the history of the world as energy giant Enron fell. The company has collapsed after it was found to have disguised billions of dollars of debt, leading an outraged Senate to call for an immediate investigation.

Scene Two/Three – Circle of Blame

The detritus of an unexpected fall litters the stage. Order must be restored.

Trials/hearings.

Senator   These hearings are an attempt to investigate America's largest corporate bankruptcy. What happened, why did it happen and who is responsible for it happening?

Those responsible are present around the outskirts of the stage, maybe some sort of a circle: **Lay,** **Fastow,** **Ramsay** *and* **Hewitt, Arthur Andersen,** *the* **Board.** *But not* **Skilling.**

A light moves from player to player as they speak.

Member of the Board (*as a statement*)   The Board is shocked and dismayed by events. We are not lawyers and had no idea Mr Fastow was doing anything illegal.

Ramsay   As a law firm, we had a responsibility to the law.

Hewitt   If illegal practises went on –

Ramsay   *After* we signed off on LJM

Hewitt   That's entirely another matter –

Ramsay   Another matter entirely.

Ramsay and Hewitt   We explicitly avoided the illegal.

Hewitt   We are not accountants.

Arthur Andersen   I am an accountant. For my sins(!)

These procedures were unusual.

Little Arthur   They were *not* illegal.

Arthur Andersen   Arthur Andersen are happy to provide all Enron-related documents.

Little Arthur   Except for all the ones we shredded.

Arthur Andersen *wrestles his dummy into acquiescence.*

Fastow   Mr Chairman, on the advice of my counsel, I respectfully decline to answer the questions put to me based on the protection afforded me under the United States Constitution.

Lay   I have been instructed by my counsel not to testify based on my fifth amendment constitutional rights.

Skilling   I will testify. I'll answer any question you got. I'll take a lie detector test right here, right now. This whole situation's been terrible for a lot of people, and I'm here to explain what happened. And how I can help.

Senator   With due respect, Mr Skilling, I'm not going to ask you to help. Let me put something to you: Is it a matter of coincidence that a few months after you left Enron the company collapsed?

Skilling   When I left Enron corporation, on August 14th of the year 2001, I believed that the company was in – was in great shape.

Senator   Do you have personal worth of more than a hundred million dollars?

Skilling   I don't have the records with me.

Senator   Would it be surprising to you to learn that you had that?

Skilling   No, that would – that would not be a surprise.

Senator   And how do you feel about the employees whose families have lost their life savings?

Skilling   Well, I guess –

Senator   You donated any of that money to employees?

Skilling   At this point I have … thirty-six separate law suits against me. It is my expectation that I will spend the next five to ten years of my life battling those lawsuits.

Senator   And you don't believe you've done anything wrong?

Skilling   The markets were … destroyed after September 11th. There were allegations of accounting problems, of accounting irregularities. In business terms, that's tantamount to yelling fire in a crowded theatre. It becomes a run on the bank.

Senator Judge (*to us*)   Thank you, Mr Skilling.

A few bad apples have shamed American corporate culture here today and I find it scandalous that he could turn up here hoping to make it the Jeff Skilling show. Well today is *our* day … Day for the US senate, the courts. And the people. And we will see that those millionaires with their private jets and luxury lifestyles are forced to explain to those of us with normal lives on the ground what misdeeds have been done. The American Government will not stand for corporate crime on this scale. I mean, on any scale.

Skilling   That was a show! Democrats trying to win votes from poor people they've never fucking met.

Lawyer   It's irrelevant now. It's about the trial.

Skilling   Well fuck them, fuck the trial and fuck America!

Lawyer   I take it we're pleading not guilty?

Skilling   I'm gonna fight this thing till the day I die.

Lawyer   What about your CFO?

Skilling   Andy's blood runs Enron, he's gonna be as mad as me.

Lawyer   Jeff, if Andy's got a lawyer half as good as me, hell, if Andy's got a lawyer who can read, he's gonna be telling him one thing – he's gonna be telling him to blame it on you.

Gavel bang three times. Trial.

Lawyer   Mr Fastow, you've spent a great deal of time today describing your actions as a 'hero of Enron'. Do you really view your behaviour as heroic?

Fastow   I think I said I was a hero and I believed I was a hero in the context of Enron's culture.

Lawyer   You must be consumed by an insatiable greed, is that fair to say?

Fastow   I believe I was extremely greedy and lost my moral compass. I've done terrible things that I very much regret.

Lawyer   That sounded awfully rehearsed, Mr Fastow.

Fastow   With respect, your questions sound pretty rehearsed too.

Lawyer 2   Are you smart, Mr Skilling?

Skilling   Yes.

Lawyer 2   Sure you are. So you knew and understood what Mr Fastow was doing at your company?

Fastow   We knew and understood that it was wrong.

Skilling   I knew and understood that it was legal.

Lawyer   Did you steal?

Fastow   We stole. We all benefitted financially.

Skilling   I would never steal from Enron.

Lawyer   Did you profit personally, illegally from LJM?

Fastow   Yes, I did.

Skilling   I did not know that.

Lawyer 2   You did not *want* to know.

Lawyer   How much?

Fastow   It's difficult to say.

Lawyer   Try.

Fastow   Around forty-five million dollars /.

Lawyer   / Forty-five million(!)

And how much did Mr Skilling profit personally?

Skilling   None.

Fastow   None. *Directly.*

Lawyer   None! So doesn't it make sense that you'd protect yourself today? Say anything to get your boss convicted, maybe make arrangements with the federal government!

Lawyer 2   Objection!

Lawyer   He promoted you, supported you and trusted you, did not profit at all yet was betrayed by you!

Lawyer 2   Mr Skilling, During the period of February '99 through June 2001 did you convert your stock worth sixty-six million dollars?

Skilling   That sounds –

Lawyer 2   All the time telling employees to invest?

Fastow   When you misrepresent the nature of your company –

Skilling   I believed in Enron.

Fastow   Then cash in your stock options, that is stealing –

Lawyer   We all know you know 'bout stealing, Mr Fastow –

Fastow   He committed crimes at Enron.

Lawyer   No, you committed crimes at Enron!

Lawyer 2   You thought the company was fine, everything was fine, with things in such great shape, why did you resign?

Skilling   I resigned because the market demanded it.

Lawyer 2   You left a sinking ship! Women and children first, right after Jeff!

Skilling   The company was worth what it was worth *because* of me.

Lawyer 2   Does that include the nothing it's worth now?

Beat.

Lawyer   When the history books are written about what happened at Enron you know your name is going to be on that page. You want to make sure Mr Skilling's name is on that page also.

Fastow   You know what I'd like written on that page? That I had the courage to admit I did something wrong.

Judge   Andrew Fastow, you are found guilty on two counts of criminal conspiracy.

Kenneth Lay, you are found guilty on six counts of conspiracy and securities fraud.

Lay *and* **Fastow** *are cuffed.* **Skilling** *is cuffed.*

Judge   Jeffrey Skilling, you have been found guilty of nineteen separate counts of securities fraud, wire fraud and insider trading.

Fastow *and* **Skilling** *share a look before* **Fastow** *abandons his former boss, leaving* **Skilling** *alone.*

Skilling   *You – you* failed *me*. You didn't believe enough. Don't you see? This is my life!

A funeral cortège of former employees engulfs him.

Scene Four – The Funeral

Black umbrellas go up. We're outside. Before a funeral.

Guests in mourning black gather. **Claudia Roe** *enters in mourning black;* **Skilling** *sees her.*

Skilling   Claudia.

Skilling *is escorted by a* **Police Officer** *in a suit and dark glasses.*

Skilling   Can you just give me a minute?

Police Officer   I can stand over there.

Skilling   Then could you do that please?

He does.

Roe   I didn't think they'd let you come.

Skilling   Dispensation. For an hour.

Roe   Did they tell you what happened?

Skilling   To Ken? Heart failure.

Roe   Yeah, that's the official verdict anyway. I heard you're gonna appeal.

Skilling   I told my daughter I was innocent. I believe I'm innocent.

Roe   Neither of those things make you innocent. Is it true, when it fell – the only part of the business with any worth at all was my division? The things you could hold?

Skilling   You got out!

Roe   Not by choice.

Skilling   Well, aren't you gonna thank me!?

Irene Gant, *a more mature woman, approaches* **Skilling**.

Irene Gant   Mr Skilling? My name is Irene Gant. I worked for Enron for twenty-five years. I did everything you asked. I took all my savings and I invested them in the company I worked for. I've lost a hundred and fifty thousand dollars. I have no money to retire on. And I'm living at my sister's. I wanted you to know because I swore, if I ever saw you in person, well, I don't wanna say.

Skilling   What do you expect me to say to that?

Irene Gant   I want an answer from you –

Skilling   I don't have any answers.

Irene Gant   I have lost everything!

Roe   This is not the place –

Irene Gant   Oh, am I embarrassing you? I'm sorry, am I embarrassing you?! /

Security Guard *from earlier scene approaches the hubbub.*

Security Officer   There trouble here?

Skilling   No.

The **Security Officer** *glares at* **Skilling**. **Skilling** *recognises him.*

Security Officer   There you are.

Skilling   I should go wait in the car.

Security Officer   Do you know who I am?

Skilling   Yes. You're a security officer.

Security Officer (*shakes head*)   I was.

You know what you are? You an ordinary crook. Doesn't matter how you dress it up. Nothing special about it. Took a lot of people down is all.

Skilling   It's called equity for a reason. Everyone shares what's left.

Security Officer   Everything's gone. A future of a certain kind is gone.

Skilling   I understand you're angry. And you're looking for somebody to blame.

Irene Gant   Won't even apologize.

Irene *spits at him. The* **Security Officer** *ushers* **Irene Gant** *back into the funeral throng.*

Roe   That guy's not here to stop you running. He's here to stop you getting hurt.

Skilling   Can I walk in with you?

Roe   I got to take care of myself here.

Beat.

Baptist church bells. **Roe** *leaves to enter the church alone.*

Skilling *is left alone watching the employees enter the church. He eventually turns to leave.*

Epilogue

During this chorus section, **Skilling** *changes into prison garb and hands in his possessions.*

You may wish to intersperse **Skilling***'s speech with the chorus comments, rather than playing them one after the other.*

Board   When Enron was declared bankrupt, they were over thirty billion dollars in debt.

Security Officer   Days before employees were told to leave, the latest round of bonus cheques was handed out to Enron executives, more than fifty-five million dollars.

Employee   That week alone, twenty thousand employees lost their jobs.

Senator   The financial practises pioneered at Enron are now widespread throughout the business world.

Business Analyst (Elise)   Over the last two years, the US Government has pumped over ten trillion dollars into the financial system to try and keep it from collapse.

Sloman   Counting that amount at a dollar a second would take more than 320,000 years.

Employee   Kenneth Lay was found dead in his Aspen ski-home prior to being sentenced for his crimes.

News Reporter (Gayle)   Andy Fastow received a reduced sentence of six years in minimum security in exchange for testifying against his former boss.

Lawyer   Jeffrey Skilling was sentenced to twenty-four years and four months in prison. His case is going to the Supreme Court.

Skilling (*to us*)   I'm not a bad man. I'm not an unusual man. I just wanted to change the world. And I think there'll come a time when everyone understands that. They'll realize they were banishing something of themselves along with me. I believe that.

I know it's hard to understand. How can something be worth a million dollars in the morning and nothing by the afternoon? Same way a man goes from captain of all industry to a fraud sitting in jail. You want to look at something and know it has. . . a worth, a fundamental value? Bullshit. You wanna hold a mirror up to nature?

The huge crack along the wall of the building glows from behind and becomes the jagged line graph of the Dow Jones Index over the last century.

The line on the graph/the crack glows.

Skilling (*to us*)   There's your mirror. Every dip, every crash, every bubble that's burst, that's you. Your brilliant stupidity. This one gave us the railroads. This one the internet. This one the slave trade. And if you wanna do anything about saving the environment or reaching other worlds, you'll need a bubble for that too. Everything I've ever done in my life worth anything has been done in a bubble; in a state of extreme hope and trust and stupidity. Would you have had kids if you'd known the true pain of them arriving, and then of them leaving? Would you have gotten married if you could see her face twenty years on turn to you through tears and say, 'You never knew me at all'?

Skilling *points to spikes and dips on the graph.*

Skilling   All humanity is here. There's Greed, there's Fear, Joy, Faith … Hope …

And the greatest of these … is Money.

The sound of prison doors slamming.

The End.